PROTECT OUR PLANET

Take action with Romário

Published by Struik Nature
(an imprint of Penguin Random House South Africa (Pty) Ltd)
Reg. No. 1953/000441/07
The Estuaries No. 4, Oxbow Crescent, Century Avenue, Century City, 7441
PO Box 1144, Cape Town, 8000 South Africa

Visit www.penguinrandomhouse.co.za and join the Struik Nature Club
for updates, news, events and special offers.

First published in 2022
1 3 5 7 9 10 8 6 4 2

Publisher: Pippa Parker
Managing editor: Roelien Theron
Compiler and project manager: Heléne Booyens
Designers: Heléne Booyens, Neil Bester, Gillian Black
Picture researcher: Colette Stott
Proofreader: Emsie du Plessis

Reproduction by Studio Repro
Printed and bound by Shumani RSA, Parow, Cape Town

ISBN 978 1 77584 823 3 (Print)
ISBN 978 1 77584 824 0 (ePub)

Mapula
Trust

The Publishers are grateful for the kind sponsorship
of this project by the Mapula Trust.

CONTENTS

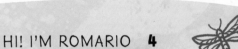

Hi! I'M ROMARIO

I'm an eco-warrior from Durban, South Africa. I love planting trees, cleaning the beach, and making art. I want to be a scientist to better understand the natural world.

MY ORCA OUTFIT!

My journey started at a school play about the ocean. My classmates dressed up as sharks, starfish, octopi and crabs. I found out that all these wonderful sea creatures are in danger because of pollution. So, I decided to become an activist and protect nature.

I live next to the sea. Every weekend, I clean the beach. I want to look after this special place, because I love living here. I get to surf with the fish and watch bottlenose dolphins and huge whales, which is super amazing!

I use my mum's kitchen sieve to sift **NURDLES** from the sand. Nurdles are tiny plastic pellets. Read more about them on page 35.

BOTTLENOSE DOLPHIN

TURTLES ARE MY FAVOURITE SEA CREATURES

Trees are wonders of nature. They give us fruit to eat, wood to build with, and clean air to breathe (see how on page 43). I save my pocket money and raise funds to plant trees all over the world. The more trees, the better – unless they're aliens (find out why on page 47).

I'VE PLANTED **450** TREES IN **27** COUNTRIES

PEPPERBARK TREES

(see how on page 43)
(find out why on page 47)

Art is my passion. My mum is an artist, and taught me how to paint when I was five years old. I like painting birds with colourful plumage. I usually pick endangered species, such as penguins and parrots, because art can be a powerful way of teaching people about conservation.

Romario

I am an ornithophile – I love birds! They are bright and beautiful, their singing and tweeting make me happy, and they help the ecosystem in many, many ways. My favourite bird is the hoopoe – it has a striking crown of black-tipped feathers on its head and a zebra pattern on its body. To protect endangered birds, I do fundraising campaigns (read more on page 15).

(read more on page 15)

HOOPOE

My HOBBIES

CHESS

HOCKEY

CODING

GARDENING

WATCHING MYSTERY MOVIES

SWIMMING

RUNNING

I want to LEARN HOW TO

SANDBOARD

PLAY GUITAR

COME WITH ME
to discover how you can become an eco-warrior!

BUBBLES OF LIFE

The natural world is made up of ecosystems: that is, all the living creatures and the non-living elements in a specific area, as well as what happens between them. Find out how these 'bubbles of life' work, and why they must be kept stable.

Knysna forest

CRITICAL CONNECTIONS

Ecosystems consist of a complex web of interactions. In the African savanna, for instance, lions work as a team to hunt antelope, hyenas steal cheetah kills, dung beetles lay their eggs in elephant droppings and oxpeckers pick the ticks from other animals. Non-living elements are important too: soil is essential for healthy plant growth, rain fills waterholes where crocodiles lie in wait, and rocks and mounds provide sun-basking spots for lizards and other reptiles.

African savanna

Namib Desert

ECOSYSTEMS CAN BE AS BIG AS A DESERT, OR AS SMALL AS A PUDDLE IN THE ROAD.

The African elephant is a **KEYSTONE** species in the savanna ecosystem: its activities are essential for the survival of other species. Elephants eat and trample so much vegetation that they prevent the savanna from turning into a forest.

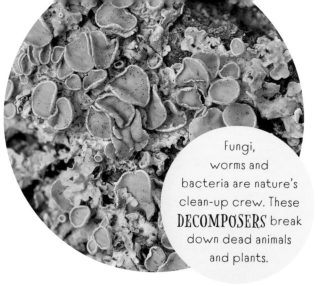

Fungi, worms and bacteria are nature's clean-up crew. These **DECOMPOSERS** break down dead animals and plants.

SMALL BUT SIGNIFICANT

Insects play a very important role in all ecosystems. They carry pollen between male and female flowers, essential for seed development. They are a source of food for bigger animals. They tunnel through soil, keeping it from becoming too compact.

A beetle spreads pollen from flower to flower as it feeds.

CATASTROPHIC CHANGES

Since all the living and non-living things in an ecosystem are linked, disturbing the balance of even one element can have serious effects. Dumping toxic waste in a river will not only kill the fish, but also poison the animals that feed on them. Harvesting too many flowers leaves nectar-feeding birds and insects without food. Killing snakes will cause the rat population to grow, because fewer snakes will be hunting rats.

WETLAND ECOSYSTEMS PROVIDE BREEDING GROUNDS FOR A VARIETY OF CREATURES.

Wetland ecosystems are very sensitive. To monitor wetland health, scientists keep an eye on **INDICATOR** species - those that react to changes first.

Humans have created something new: **URBAN ECOSYSTEMS,** where creatures such as rats, cockroaches and pigeons have adapted to life in the city.

UNDERWATER ECOSYSTEMS

Corals look like rocky plants, but are actually colonies of thousands of tiny animals with outer skeletons of limestone. They form large reefs that teem with marine life: numerous fish, clams, crabs, sponges and sea stars live in these special underwater ecosystems.

Our planet's
NATURAL RESOURCES

Diamond rings, rocket fuel and chicken nuggets are all made from **NATURAL RESOURCES**. Like fresh air and fruit trees, they are provided by nature. Read on to discover some of Earth's greatest gifts.

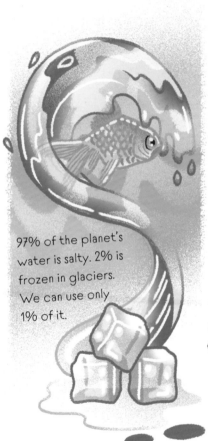

97% of the planet's water is salty. 2% is frozen in glaciers. We can use only 1% of it.

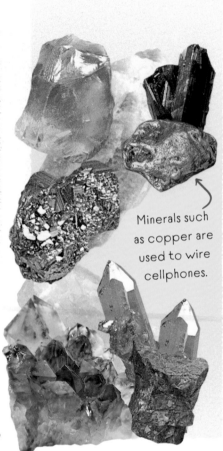

Minerals such as copper are used to wire cellphones.

WATER

Every living thing needs water to survive. We also use it to cultivate crops, grow gardens, cook food, clean up, cool down, produce electricity and power factories. Since most of the planet's water is salty, we need to keep our precious freshwater sources clean.

MINERALS

Gold, diamonds and iron ore are a few of the well-known minerals dug out of the ground. Some minerals, such as quartz crystals, are fashioned into jewellery. Others, like tungsten, are made into building tools. Everything, from coins to car parts, began as raw minerals.

FOSSIL FUELS

Oil, coal and natural gas are all fossil fuels. They were formed deep underground from the remains of plants and animals that died millions of years ago. Humans burn fossil fuels for heat and power, but burning this resource pollutes the environment.

WILL IT LAST FOREVER?

Some natural resources, such as sunlight and air, are **RENEWABLE**. They cannot be used up. Others, such as oil and coal, are **NON-RENEWABLE**. We are using them faster than they can form.

WARNING! Even renewable resources can take strain if they are heavily polluted. For example: if the sky is full of smoke, sunlight can't reach us properly.

Food crops grow back and farm animals breed, so they are technically a **RENEWABLE** resource.

Plants need sunlight to grow. They bend to face the warm rays.

Is your calculator solar-powered?

AIR

Besides moving rain clouds, spreading seeds and lifting paragliders, the wind can generate eco-friendly energy by spinning the blades of huge wind turbines. Keeping the air we breathe clean is important – dirty air can cause asthma and other lung ailments.

SUNLIGHT

The sun radiates light and heat, powering life on the planet. Sunlight is an inexhaustible source of clean energy. Solar panels absorb the sun's rays, using it to generate electricity. The sun can power everything from cars to satellites and calculators.

BIODIVERSITY

We rely on plants and animals for countless things: food and fuel, for example. Recreation is a valuable but often overlooked use of natural resources. We enjoy the wonderful biodiversity around us by birdwatching, game viewing, hiking, camping and fishing.

HUMANS AND NATURE

Until a few thousand years ago, people lived in smaller communities, using the resources in their immediate environment to survive. Everything changed with the dawn of the **INDUSTRIAL REVOLUTION,** when human impact on the planet grew at a record-breaking pace.

LIVING IN HARMONY

Early humans were hunter-gatherers, and lived in small travelling groups, not in towns or cities. They hunted animals such as antelope and buffalo, and foraged for fruit, berries, eggs, honey and other foods. Cave paintings show hunts that took place tens of thousands of years ago.

FORAGERS TO FARMERS

About ten thousand years ago, humans **DOMESTICATED** animals such as sheep, goats, cattle, pigs and dogs. That is, they kept and bred the tamest ones. They also began growing plants that were normally wild, including figs, wheat and peas. With food readily available, humans could build towns and cities instead of wandering from place to place in search of food.

THE REVOLUTION

When the steam engine was invented in the 1700s, it changed life forever. By burning coal, this engine could power everything, from factories to trains. It was the start of the **INDUSTRIAL REVOLUTION.** With steam power, people could build things quickly and cheaply in factories. More inventions followed, more roads were built, and cities grew larger and larger.

Today, much of Africa's wildlife is protected in game reserves and national parks, where they can live without being disturbed or illegally hunted by humans.

TOO MANY PEOPLE!

Since the Industrial Revolution, the number of humans on Earth has exploded. Because of improved medicine, a steady supply of food from farms, and our ability to filter and clean water, people are less likely to die young. They are also more likely to have children, so the population grows and grows. It may sound like good news, but **OVERPOPULATION** is the root of many of the problems humans cause for nature.

DESTRUCTION AND DISASTER

The larger the human population, the greater the pressure on natural resources. Natural habitats are cleared for farms, forests are chopped down for wood, coal is burned to power factories, smoke is pumped into the sky and trash is thrown into landfills. Advanced technology can also go very wrong, causing disasters such as oil spills and nuclear meltdowns.

PROTECTING THE PLANET

When humans destroy habitats, catch too many fish, poison rivers with toxic waste, or fill the oceans with rubbish, they can drive species to extinction. Since people are the problem, we also have to be the solution. Read on to discover how we are trying to solve human-made problems in nature.

GAME RESERVE

ANIMAL ACTIVISM

Before you think of starting a conservation campaign, you need to know which animals most need your help. The 'Red List' sorts species from Least Concern (plentiful in the wild) to Extinct (died out).

REVERSE THE RED!

PROTECT THE PANDA

LEAST CONCERN

The springbok is South Africa's national animal. It is abundant in the wild and doesn't face major threats. No special conservation efforts are required.

NEAR THREATENED

A beautiful marine creature, the whitespotted eagle ray will likely become endangered in the future because many are caught for display in private aquariums.

VULNERABLE

The ground pangolin is the most trafficked mammal in the world. Its unique scales are sold illegally and used in traditional medicine, and its meat is eaten as a delicacy.

NEW HOPE FOR THE CHEETAH

Cheetahs have escaped extinction in the past. However, since only small groups of survivors remained, the gene pool was worryingly small. Cheetahs often mated with close relatives, leading to less robust offspring. To solve this problem, ecologists began trapping and relocating these big cats. This meant that cheetahs could mate with others that weren't as closely related.

Twenty years ago, the black rhino was hunted to the edge of extinction for its horn. Fewer than 2,500 remained! After intensive conservation efforts, their numbers have doubled. There is still a long way to go.

SAVE THE RHINO

Make a poster of an important endangered animal!

Poachers illegally catch or kill animals for body parts, such as hides, horns, scales, bones and teeth. Some people poach plants too, digging up rare species and selling them.

The riverine rabbit is **ENDEMIC** to the Karoo region of South Africa, meaning that it occurs nowhere else. It is critically endangered because of habitat loss.

ENDANGERED

The western leopard toad is likely to become extinct. Its natural habitat is being cleared for housing, and it must cross roads to get to breeding sites – a dangerous journey.

CRITICAL

The orangutan is an intelligent primate. It is hunted for its meat and is poached for the pet trade. It is classified as Critical, meaning that extinction is extremely likely.

EXTINCT

Dead as a dodo! This large, flightless bird lived on the island of Mauritius. When sailors arrived in the 1600s, the dodo was easy prey. It was eventually driven to extinction.

CONSERVATION CHALLENGE

When humans chop down trees or clear land for farming, giraffes struggle to find food. Scientists are researching ways to help, but there's a problem: how do you transport the world's tallest mammal to a new home? Sometimes they are transported by very large trucks, but it is slow going.

The giant panda is an **UMBRELLA** species: a popular, charismatic animal used to create awareness and drive a conservation campaign. By protecting the panda's habitat, smaller critters that live there are protected too.

BIRDS IN PERIL

Birds face unique conservation challenges, and some are in greater danger than others. To help protect birds, you need to know which groups are the most vulnerable, and why.

Great white pelican

African penguins

Bateleur

WATERBIRDS

Pelicans, herons, ducks and other waterbirds live in and around rivers and deltas. They are fascinating – some build floating nests from twigs, others construct muddy mounds to house their chicks. Water pollution, the construction of dams and noisy boats disturb their breeding and feeding.

SEABIRDS

Penguins, cormorants, albatrosses, gulls and other seabirds face threats from land *and* sea: oil spills and plastic pollution, for example. Most seabirds breed on islands, making them extra vulnerable – breeding sites are very limited, and the chicks have no way to escape predators such as cats.

RAPTORS

Predatory birds, such as eagles, hawks and owls, have large home ranges where they hunt for prey. They struggle to find food if their habitat shrinks to make space for buildings. Many scavenging birds, such as vultures, die when farmers put out poisoned bait for other problem animals such as jackals.

DANGEROUS JOURNEYS

European bee-eaters are colourful little birds. Every year, they migrate between Europe and southern Africa.

Many birds are MIGRATORY. As the seasons change, they fly to places where the conditions are best: where the weather is fine, for example, or where their insect prey will be plentiful. Some species travel thousands of kilometres between northern breeding sites and southern wintering spots.

The journey is fraught with dangers, such as bad weather, but human activity makes it even more challenging. Birds are known to crash into powerlines and television aerials. City-light pollution makes it harder to navigate. And habitat loss means birds have fewer places to rest and forage in.

PET TRADE PROBLEMS

From lovebirds and budgies to cockatoos and canaries, birds are popular pets. The African grey is one of the most well-known tame parrots. It is as smart as a four-year-old human, very talkative, and can live for over 50 years. Despite its talents, the African grey is endangered in the wild. Its natural habitat is the West and Central African rainforests, which are being cut down for timber and to make way for farms. Poachers also steal chicks and sell them to the pet trade.

BIRDS BELONG IN THEIR NATURAL HABITAT!

The **CAPE PARROT** is South Africa's only endemic parrot. It lives in forests and uses its strong beak to crack fruit kernels and nuts. Pet parrots are bred in captivity, but wild chicks are poached too.

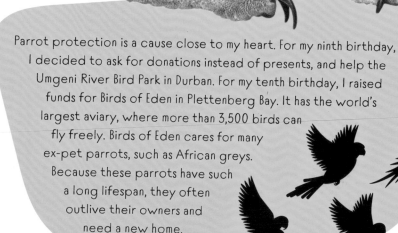

Parrot protection is a cause close to my heart. For my ninth birthday, I decided to ask for donations instead of presents, and help the Umgeni River Bird Park in Durban. For my tenth birthday, I raised funds for Birds of Eden in Plettenberg Bay. It has the world's largest aviary, where more than 3,500 birds can fly freely. Birds of Eden cares for many ex-pet parrots, such as African greys. Because these parrots have such a long lifespan, they often outlive their owners and need a new home.

UNDER OUR WING

Find out what's being done to protect endangered birds, and how you can help the feathered friends in your backyard.

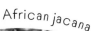

African jacana

Cape gannets

Bearded vulture

COUNTING CHICKS

When it comes to conservation, step one is collecting data: observing and regularly counting wetland birds to ensure numbers remain stable, or fitting large migratory birds with trackers. This way, scientists can identify problems and find important birds and habitats to protect.

SMART SOLUTIONS

Because threats to birds are so varied, each case requires a unique solution. When endangered Cape gannets abandoned their breeding colony, for example, conservationists worked out that bird-eating seals were the problem. They seal-proofed the site, and the birds returned.

LONG-TERM PLANS

Big raptors take a long time to grow up and raise chicks, so populations grow very slowly. The critically endangered bearded vulture is one such bird. It lays two eggs each year, but raises only one chick. Conservationists have devised a long-term plan: they remove the 'spare' egg, hatch it, and breed birds that can be released into the wild.

MY BIRD PORTRAITS

VULTURE RESTAURANTS

With their bald heads and beady eyes, vultures are not the prettiest of birds. Cleaning up carcasses is an important task, however, so these scavengers are worth protecting. People are helping vultures by setting up 'restaurants' where piles of poison-free meat are provided to sustain the birds when food is scarce. Vulture restaurants also provide an eco-friendly way to get rid of animal remains and dead livestock.

I paint colourful birds to raise awareness about endangered species. From left to right, these three are the crimson-rumped toucanet, rose-breasted cockatoo and scarlet macaw.

Why don't you paint your own bird portrait? First, find a colourful photo to use as a reference. Get a soft, light pencil and draw the outline, feathers, beak and eyes. Then grab your brushes and start painting!

MAKE A BIRDFEEDER

WHAT YOU'LL NEED
- Large, ripe orange
- Garden-bird seed mix
- Two wooden skewers
- Twine

WHAT TO DO
Slice the orange in half and scoop out the flesh with a spoon. Poke the two skewers through the bowl to form a cross. Tie the twine to the skewers, then fill the bowl with seed mix and hang it in the garden. Replace your birdfeeder after a few weeks, before it rots.

INSTALL A BIRD BATH

Birds can drink, cool down and clean their feathers in a garden bird bath. Shallow basins work best – even small birds with short legs must be able to stand in the deepest water. Place the bath somewhere where cats can't creep up. Keep it topped up with fresh water, and clean it often – don't allow algae to grow in it.

BACKYARD BIODIVERSITY

Not all our neighbours are human – we share the street with all kinds of creatures. Birds are colourful and easy to spot, but small animals such as frogs, insects and lizards are very much around us too.

FRIEND OR FOE?

Gardens are full of insects. A handful of species, such as tiny sap-sucking aphids and snout beetles, are harmful to plants, but most are helpful. Ladybird beetles are welcome in every garden – they are natural pest-controllers that prey on the 'bad' bugs, and can eat over 5,000 little aphids in their lifetime!

SCALY AND SLIMY

Have you seen geckos, skinks and other lizards basking in the sun or lying in wait for their insect prey? These cold-blooded hunters are harmless to humans, but keep pest populations in check. Frogs are a rare sight, but you might be lucky enough to hear them at night, especially when it rains. Make your garden frog-friendly by building a Toad Abode – see page 21!

The African monarch is a common butterfly with an unusual story. Its caterpillars feed on toxic milkweed leaves, but are immune to its poison. They store the toxins in their bodies, making them poisonous to eat.

The caterpillars of monarch butterflies have bright colours to warn predators that they are poisonous.

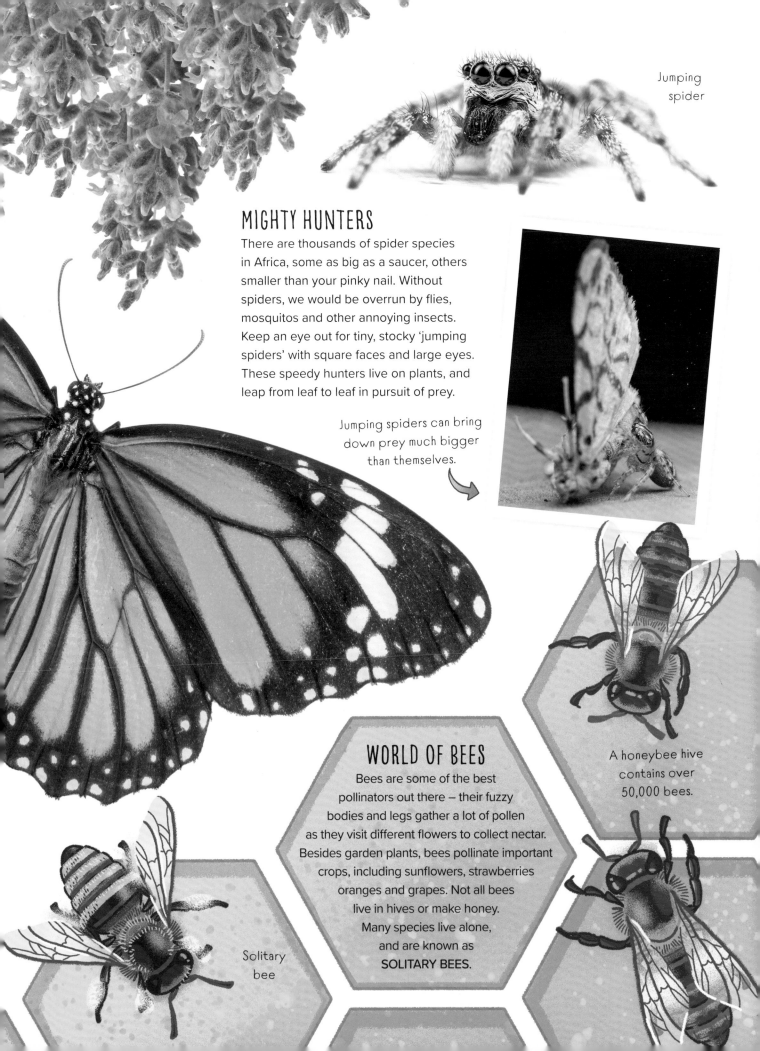

Jumping spider

MIGHTY HUNTERS

There are thousands of spider species in Africa, some as big as a saucer, others smaller than your pinky nail. Without spiders, we would be overrun by flies, mosquitos and other annoying insects. Keep an eye out for tiny, stocky 'jumping spiders' with square faces and large eyes. These speedy hunters live on plants, and leap from leaf to leaf in pursuit of prey.

Jumping spiders can bring down prey much bigger than themselves.

WORLD OF BEES

Bees are some of the best pollinators out there – their fuzzy bodies and legs gather a lot of pollen as they visit different flowers to collect nectar. Besides garden plants, bees pollinate important crops, including sunflowers, strawberries oranges and grapes. Not all bees live in hives or make honey. Many species live alone, and are known as **SOLITARY BEES.**

A honeybee hive contains over 50,000 bees.

Solitary bee

HOMEMADE HABITATS

Turn your backyard into a home for bees, beetles, spiders, slugs and other creatures by building a bug box – a mini-habitat where these creepy-crawlies can rest, breed and feed.

1. PICK THE PERFECT HOME

First, you'll need a container for your bug box. It must be able to withstand the wind and weather outdoors. An old tin can, glass jar, wooden box or flowerpot will work well. You can also cut a hole in a plastic milk container, or cut off the top of an empty soda bottle.

2. GATHER YOUR GEAR

Search outdoors to find natural materials to fill your container: twigs, bark, moss, bamboo canes, small rocks and even bits of broken ceramic flowerpots. These will help to create the nooks and crannies that creepy-crawlies love.

To decorate your bug box, you'll need scissors, twine, self-sealing acrylic paint and paintbrushes.

TWIGS

BITS OF BARK

STRAW

POTTERY PIECES

PINE CONES

BAMBOO CANES

3. FILL THE BOX

It's time to stuff the bug box! Snap twigs, break bark and cut straw to make them short enough to fit in your container. There is no wrong way to fill your bug box – you could even use a large pine cone surrounded by moss, or a tin full of bark and rocks, or a mixture of everything. Pack the box tightly, until everything is nice and firm and won't fall out easily.

Use your imagination to decorate your bug box.

4. FIND A SAFE SPOT

Find a safe, sheltered corner in the garden. Place your bug box on its side, not upright. If you choose to hang it in a tree, be sure to tie it to the branch with twine so that it won't shake and spin when the wind blows.

TOAD ABODES

Frogs need damp soil and places to hide. Make your garden frog-friendly with a small pond and shelter.

WHAT YOU'LL NEED:

- A large, round plant bowl with no hole in the bottom
- A flowerpot (ceramic is best, but plastic or metal will do)
- Medium-sized rocks
- Plant matter such as small logs, branches and moss

1. To make the pond, dig a hole and plant the round bowl.

2. Place some rocks inside and around the bowl for perches.

3. To make the shelter, half-bury the flowerpot on its side next to the bowl.

4. Place rocks around the opening of the pot, leaving a small entrance.

5. Decorate with plant matter, and fill the bowl with water. Remember to keep it topped up.

MAKING A MESS

Pollution happens when something harmful, such as litter or toxic smoke, goes into the environment and causes damage to life forms and infects the air, water and soil. Pollution takes many forms. Some are visible, as in an oil spill, but others, such as gases or noise, are invisible.

Batteries and paints release toxic chemicals into the earth.

Marine wildlife can choke when they mistake human litter for food.

UNHEALTHY AIR

Factories, power plants, planes in the sky, vehicles on the road and wildfires all release pollutants into the **AIR** that we breathe. The smoke, dust and gases are bad for our health and affect the climate too. The haze of pollution that sometimes blankets cities is known as **smog** (a combination of 'smoke' and 'fog').

SOILED EARTH

When farmers use too much pesticide to kill the insects that feed on their crops, these mixtures seep into the **SOIL** under our feet. Chemicals and oils from fertilisers and buried trash are also absorbed into the ground. Toxins can gradually build up, poisoning the soil until nothing can grow. They can also leach into the groundwater, polluting our drinkwater.

MURKY WATERS

Raw sewage dumped into rivers and dirty runoff from farms and factories pollute fresh **WATER** supplies. Pollution can make water too acidic, warm, salty or murky, and unable to support life. Dirty water can spread diseases such as cholera. In the ocean, oil spills coat and kill seabirds, shellfish, seals and other marine animals, and take months to clean up.

A sound's loudness is measured in decibels (dB). Sounds above 85dB can cause hearing loss over time.

Whisper = 30dB
Lawn mower = 90dB
Rock concert = 110dB
Fireworks = 140dB

NOISY NEIGHBOURS

Cars honking, plane engines roaring and the loud sound of a construction site all cause **NOISE** pollution. A too-noisy environment disturbs animals and can hinder people's sleep and abilty to concentrate.

Many whale and dolphin species rely on sound to navigate, hunt and communicate underwater. Offshore drilling and loud ship engines interfere with their sensitive hearing.

TOO BRIGHT!

Streetlamps, bright billboards, car headlights and other sources of artificial **LIGHT** can confuse animals that use moonlight to navigate. They can also disrupt our sleep cycles, and make stars less visible in the night sky.

Baby turtles hatch on sandy beaches. At night, they find their ocean home by heading to the brightest light they can see – usually the moonlight reflected on the water. But if coastal cities have too many lights, hatchlings could head in the wrong direction.

WASTE IN SPACE

Pollution has reached just about every part of the planet – and even the **SPACE** surrounding it. Bits of broken spacecraft and satellites orbit the Earth. Many of the scattered pieces are small, but they travel at extreme speeds, posing a danger to other space missions.

NASA keeps track of thousands of space junk pieces, some as small as a marble, to prevent collisions with spacecraft.

Understanding CLIMATE CHANGE

How does pollution cause the weather to change, the sea level to rise, and deserts to spread? It's a long story – let's start at the beginning.

A greenhouse is a building made of glass, used to grow plants and protect them from the cold.

During the day, sunlight shines through the glass and heats up the air inside the greenhouse. The glass walls trap the heat inside, keeping the plants warm, even at night. We call this the

GREENHOUSE EFFECT

The same thing happens on our planet. Instead of a layer of glass, Earth is surrounded by an atmosphere of gases.

These gases include methane, carbon dioxide and water vapour, and are known as

GREENHOUSE GASES

When light from the sun passes through the atmosphere and heats up the planet, greenhouse gases keep the heat from leaking out to space.

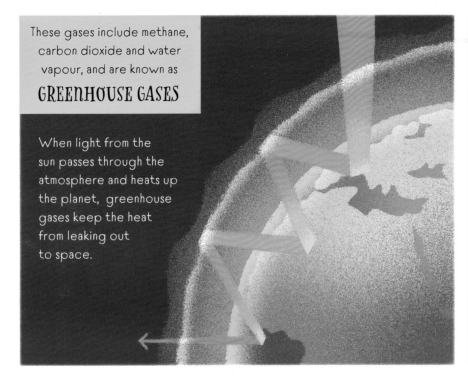

So, greenhouse gases are a good thing. Without them...

...Earth would be frozen solid.

BRRRR...

A greenhouse gas becomes a problem when there is **TOO MUCH** of it in the atmosphere. This happens when humans. . .

...burn fossil fuels

(to power our cities, electronics and cars)

...chop down trees

(because trees take carbon out of the atmosphere)

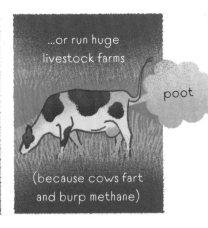

...or run huge livestock farms

poot

(because cows fart and burp methane)

As more gases are released into the atmosphere, trapping more heat, the planet gets warmer. This is known as

GLOBAL WARMING

Global warming causes sea ice and glaciers to melt. This water flows into the ocean, making the sea level rise.

Rising temperatures mess with the weather patterns, causing

CLIMATE CHANGE

Climate change has many, many different effects, such as...

Severe storms

Unseasonal weather

Prolonged drought

Coral bleaching

(because the ocean is too warm)

Wildfires

Crop failure

Extinction
(because species can't cope)

There's still a lot we don't know.

How far will sea levels rise?

How many species will go extinct?

One thing **IS** certain. We must **TAKE ACTION** to stop climate change from further harming the planet and its ecosystems.

The international community has pledged to reduce greenhouse gas emissions.

But you can help too – see how on page 26.

How to shrink your CARBON FOOTPRINT

Many activities, such as travel, watching television and washing clothes, use energy that is produced by burning fossil fuels. Burning fuel releases carbon dioxide and other greenhouse gases. Every person has a **CARBON FOOTPRINT**: that is, the amount of carbon dioxide pumped into the atmosphere to meet their energy needs as they go about their day. Here's what you can do to reduce *your* footprint:

FLIP THE SWITCH. It's simple: turn the lights off when you leave the room. This small action can have a big impact. Join the Earth Hour movement on the last Saturday of every March, when people across the planet switch off their lights and use the hour of darkness to raise awareness about climate change.

UNPLUG ENERGY VAMPIRES. Many older chargers use electricity even when they are not connected to laptops and phones. When you're not using them, unplug them completely. Don't leave a computer on screensaver for hours – switch it off instead.

EAT IN. Restaurant meals have a larger carbon footprint than home-cooked food, because a business needs to light and heat a whole building. Learn to prepare your own meals – try out the recipe on page 51.

Pets also have a carbon footprint! See page 39.

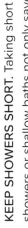

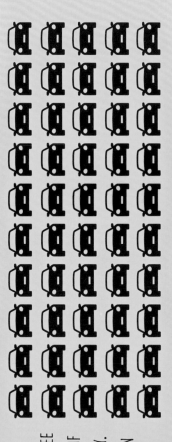

LED

Incandescent

Which bulbs light up your home? **INCANDESCENT** bulbs have curls of wire inside, and are an old design. **LED** bulbs are newer technology. They last longer and use less energy.

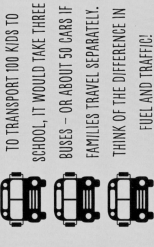

DO YOUR CHORES PROPERLY. Don't start the washing machine before it's full – it'll do half the work but use the same amount of energy required for a full load. Washing with cold water rather than warm water uses less energy. Instead of putting wet clothes in a tumble dryer, hang them in the sun to dry.

KEEP SHOWERS SHORT. Taking short showers or shallow baths not only saves water, but also the power used to heat it. If you're brave enough, use cold water – at least on hot summer days!

AVOID THE AIRCON. Cooling a room with an air conditioner uses a lot of electricity. If you can do without it – great! If it's simply too hot, remember that a fan uses less power and is more eco-friendly.

TIDY THE FRIDGE. The more disorganised the fridge is, the longer the door has to stay open while you look for what you want, letting cold air escape. It takes energy to cool everything down again. Another tip: do not put hot food directly into the fridge – wait until it cools.

WHY CARPOOL?

Driving pollutes the environment. It's not always possible to walk or cycle to the shop or school, but sharing cars or travelling by bus can also make a huge difference. It saves fuel, reduces emissions and causes less traffic.

TO TRANSPORT 100 KIDS TO SCHOOL, IT WOULD TAKE THREE BUSES – OR ABOUT 50 CARS IF FAMILIES TRAVEL SEPARATELY. THINK OF THE DIFFERENCE IN FUEL AND TRAFFIC!

FACE THE WASTE

Almost everything we do, buy or eat leaves some kind of trash behind. Shockingly, just one-tenth of our rubbish is recycled. The rest is burned, buried or dumped in the ocean.

WASHED-UP RUBBISH

WHERE'S IT FROM?

Households are not the biggest culprits when it comes to creating waste. In fact, almost 90% of rubbish is created elsewhere: building sites leave old bricks and broken tiles behind, shops throw packaging material away, hospitals dispose of used medical tools, and miners dump sand and slush as they dig – to name just a few.

PLASTIC TRASH

PLASTIC IS USEFUL, CHEAP AND EASY TO MAKE. IT WAS INVENTED ABOUT 110 YEARS AGO, BUT WILL POLLUTE THE PLANET FOR THOUSANDS MORE. IT NEVER ROTS, IT JUST SLOWLY BREAKS INTO SMALLER AND SMALLER BITS.

SHOPPING BAGS

MOULDY STRAWBERRIES

ROTTING RUBBISH

Over time, garbarge breaks down, or **DECOMPOSES**. Think of rusty cars falling apart, or fruit going mouldy. If something is **BIODEGRADABLE**, it can be broken down by living organisms, such as fungi. An apple takes two months to decompose completely. Woollen socks take five years, and car tyres over 2,000 years.

TERRIBLE TRASH PITS

USED CAR TYRES

Landfills are massive rubbish dumps where trash is buried. They come with many problems. Animal habitats are destroyed to make room for them. Disease-carrying rats move in. Dangerous gases form as many things rot at the same time (and stink). Toxins seep into the soil.

OLD BATTERIES

When batteries die for good, they shouldn't be thrown out with the rest of the trash. Even small TV remote batteries can start fires because they overheat when the negative and positive posts touch metal. Many batteries contain harmful chemicals such as lead, lithium and sulfuric acid. Dispose of old batteries at special recycling points.

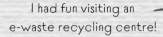

ELECTRONIC WASTE

In a world where new smartphone, tablet and laptop models are developed every year, disposing of electronic waste (e-waste) is a growing problem. Appliances like microwaves, printers, fridges and lamps also fall under e-waste. These electronics contain dangerous materials that can harm the environment if they leak out. Many appliances contain valuable elements such as copper, tin, silver and even gold. That's why all e-waste should be sent to special recycling facilities. A parent or teacher can look online to locate the nearest centre.

POLLUTION SOLUTIONS

Humans need to produce less waste. It's time for a lifestyle change! Use the eco-friendly **FIVE Rs** to keep new things from being made and old things from becoming rubbish.

THE FIVE Rs

1. REFUSE
The first step to cutting down on waste is saying NO to what you don't need. Buy second-hand goods rather than new ones – from electronics to vintage clothes. Choose products that don't come with a lot of packaging. Avoid single-use items, such as take-away cutlery.

Say no to plastic straws! Millions wind up in the ocean.

2. REDUCE
Do clothes you've outgrown clutter your cupboard? Are old toys and electronics gathering dust? Somebody out there will gladly use what you no longer need. By selling (or donating) old or unused possessions, fewer things need to be made from brand new material.

3. REUSE
Make your belongings last as long as possible. Before binning or replacing something, see if it can be repaired or repurposed. Mend torn clothing and fix frayed headphone cords, for example. See page 40 for a fun project idea using old paper.

4. RECYCLE
If you can't refuse, reduce or reuse, it's time to recycle. Throw old paper, plastic, glass and metal into their respective recycling bins so that they can be remade into something new. Recycling takes less energy and fewer resources than making something from scratch.

5. ROT
Don't just throw your leftovers in the bin – put them back into the earth! In a landfill, decaying organic waste creates the greenhouse gas methane (and smells terrible!). Instead, compost your scraps to create a nutrient-rich fertiliser for your garden.

Read more about composting on page 53!

An aluminium soda can could be recycled within a few weeks. But if it's dumped in a landfill, it takes over 200 years to break down!

WHAT CAN (AND CAN'T) YOU RECYCLE?

Search for the recycling symbol on the bottom of an item before you throw it away.

Remember to remove metal lids and plastic caps from glass bottles.

If a pizza box is oily, it can't be recycled.

sticky notes

Plastic with food on it can't be recycled. Rinse it first!

Window panes take extra long to melt, so not many places can recycle them.

PAPER

The more paper you recycle, the fewer trees are cut down to make paper products.

PLASTIC

Many plastics can't be recycled. The best thing to do is not to use much plastic in the first place.

GLASS

Glass can be melted and reshaped into new products over and over, with no loss in quality.

SAVE OUR SEAS

Oceans cover more than two-thirds of the Earth's surface. Most of this underwater world is unexplored, and many marine species still await discovery. It is important to protect this special part of our planet.

WORKING WITH WATER

Oceanographers are scientists who study underwater wildlife, tides and currents, and the trenches and mountains on the sea floor. Their work helps to protect underwater habitats such as coral reefs, seagrass meadows and kelp forests. Understanding the ocean is important work. Oceans affect the weather, bringing cool fog or violent storms. They also create millions of jobs for people, from sailors to scuba divers, and feed billions more.

KELP FORESTS

Kelp is seaweed that forms tall underwater forests, home to hundreds of marine species. This slimy seaweed is useful to humans too: it contains a special thickening agent used in toothpaste, shampoo, ice cream, tomato sauce and puddings.

Kelp forests teem with life, from jellyfish, limpets and sea urchins to rockfish and salmon. Sharks and seals swim through them in search of food, and seabirds dive in from above to snatch fish.

When trash ends up in the ocean, it can be eaten by birds, fish, turtles and other sea creatures. They can mistake bits of plastic for fish eggs, or floating plastic bags for jellyfish. These plastic snacks can choke animals or block their stomachs, causing a slow death.

To keep warm in icy waters, whale bodies are blanketed in a thick layer of fat, called blubber. In the past, people hunted whales using huge spearguns, known as harpoons, and used oil from the blubber to make lamp fuel and soap. Today, whale hunting is banned in most countries.

OVERFISHING

Will the ocean ever run out of fish? Overfishing happens when people fish **UNSUSTAINABLY** – they catch so many fish so quickly that the species doesn't have time to recover. To keep fish species (such as tuna) from disappearing, governments make laws to control fishing.

A BAD REPUTATION

The oceans house more than 500 shark species. Some, like the great white, are top predators; others, like the tiny African lanternshark, are the ocean's clean-up crew. Sharks have a reputation as man-eaters – but worldwide, sharks bite fewer than 100 people each year. More people are injured driving to the beach than by sharks in the sea.

GHOST GEAR

One of the greatest threats to marine life is discarded fishing nets, lines and rope, also known as **GHOST GEAR**. Unsuspecting seals, whales, dolphins, seabirds, sea turtles and sharks get tangled up and killed in old fishing gear. Dropping a torn net overboard might not seem like a big deal, but it can drift through the ocean for years.

COASTAL CLEAN-UPS

Beaches are more than stretches of sand where land and sea meet – they are complicated ecosystems full of life. Keeping our coasts clean is important, since litter can disturb beach biodiversity.

Junk dumped in the sea deliberately is known as **JETSAM**, whereas **FLOTSAM** is material lost by accident. Not all beach litter comes from the ocean – a lot is washed down from the land via storm drains or rivers.

BEACH CREATURES

Shorebirds, seals and crabs are easy to see, but the beach is home to many tiny creatures as well, such as snails and beetles. Some worms are so small that they can live between grains of sand. They form an important part of the food chain.

HARDY DUNE FLORA

Life on a dune can be harsh – the sun is sweltering, the sand doesn't hold water well, and the winds are strong. Nevertheless, some of South Africa's coastal dunes are home to fynbos, smalls succulents and other hardy plants found nowhere else.

Don't pick up souvenir shells without first checking for crab inhabitants!

ALONG THE SEASHORE

Driftwood and other things that float are often left behind by the waves as the tide retreats. Be sure to pick up any plastic, but leave behind dead fish, bits of crab and washed-up jellyfish – they are bound to be scooped up by a hungry scavenger.

WHEN SHARDS OF GLASS ARE TUMBLED BY WAVES FOR MANY YEARS, THEY ARE WORN INTO SMOOTH PEBBLES KNOWN AS 'SEA GLASS'.

MESSY MICROPLASTICS

Nurdles are the building blocks of plastic products. These small plastic pellets can be shaped into anything from coat hangers to toothbrushes. Containers of nurdles occasionally fall overboard when ships are caught in storms. Millions of nurdles then drift across the oceans, washing up on beaches around the world. Tiny bits of plastic, some even smaller than flakes of glitter, are known as microplastics. These days, they are found everywhere, even at the bottom of the ocean.

NURDLES

SIFTING NURDLES FROM THE SAND

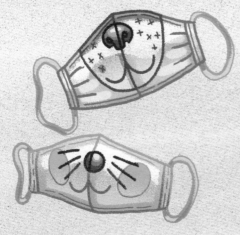

TANGLED TRASH

Since the COVID-19 pandemic, disposable face masks have become a big part of what we throw away every day. When you do throw a mask away, be sure to cut the straps so that sea creatures don't get tangled up in them. Reusable cloth masks are better for the environment.

ROMARIO'S BEACH BASICS

Every weekend, I go to the beach to pick up litter. You could do the same! Here's what you'll need:

- At least four trash bags (biodegradable bags are best), because you never know how much rubbish you will find. I've picked up plastic bottles, straws, disposable cups, nurdles, beer bottles, cigarettes, hair extensions, plastic toys that children leave on the beach, flip flops and lots of broken plastic pieces. Once, I found a creepy doll with no hands!
- A cap and strong sunscreen
- Water to drink
- A kitchen sieve for nurdle collection
- Gloves for grabbing trash

GREASY CATASTROPHE

Every now and then, ships spill oil into the sea, poisoning the water and harming marine life. The oil forms a thick layer on the surface of the water, blocking sunlight to underwater plants and seaweed. Cleaning an oil spill is a huge undertaking. Sometimes the oil is set alight on the water to burn it away. Another way of removing oil is to scoop the slick from the surface.

When the fur or feathers of marine creatures are coated in oil, they can no longer keep warm and dry. Oil spills can cause animals to freeze to death in the cold waters of the ocean.

DON'T TOUCH BROKEN GLASS – ASK AN ADULT TO DEAL WITH SHARP ITEMS.

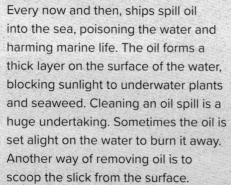

SCRAPBOOK STORIES

Here are a few favourite photos and stories from my adventures in activism! I've met interesting people (and animals), seen my trees grow and learned lots of new things about the environment, conservation and global clean-ups.

Snorkelling at uShaka Marine World in Durban. I saw a spotted unicornfish, smooth-hound shark and batfish.

I planted a coral tree in a park near my home. It's an indigenous and fast-growing species and has doubled in height in only ten months!

NOW

THEN

I met Maia, a young green sea turtle, at uShaka. She'd lost most of her front flipper after getting tangled in a plastic sack. But luckily, she was rescued and nursed back to health. I was amazed at how gracefully Maia swam with only three flippers. She was cheeky and playful, and it made me happy to see her fighting spirit. Her name means 'courage' in Māori.

Recently, I learned about **BIOMIMICRY**: imitating nature to solve human problems. For example: Japanese bullet trains made loud booms when they entered tunnels. But scientists noted kingfishers dive into water with hardly a splash. So, they reshaped the train to match the bird's streamlined beak and reduce the noise.

My dad showed me how to plant lettuce in my veggie garden.

DID YOU KNOW that tons and tons of flip flops wash up on Africa's beaches each year? They are the cheapest shoes, so many people buy them, but they last only a year or two before being thrown away. I am an ambassador of Ocean Sole, a Kenyan organisation with a special mission. They collect washed up flip flops, clean them, and create beautiful, colourful sculptures – like this zebra and lion!

Me with my friends Jinwoo (left) and Junseok on their first clean-up.

Children from Sibanesezwe Primary School in Bulawayo, Zimbabwe, plant guava trees that I sponsored through the Green Hut Trust.

MY FAVOURITE NEWS STORY

One of the largest clean-ups in history is now under way. The Great Pacific Garbage Patch is a famous 'island' of floating rubbish. Scientists are using the very latest technology to find the problem areas and clean them up, bit by bit.

Two ships drag a huge net through the ocean to collect floating plastic.

The net from above

37

SMART SHOPPING

What's on your shopping list? The things we do or don't buy can make a big difference to the environment.

Rule number one: don't buy things you don't need! Especially if they are made of plastic, which will remain on Earth for hundreds and even thousands of years.

TIME TO DEPLASTIFY

Here's a challenge: For one day, count how many pieces of plastic you throw away, such as cups, cutlery, bottles, sweet wrappers and other pieces of packaging. The next day, aim to get that number down. Avoid buying things with useless packaging. Choose reusable items: use a long-lasting cloth bag instead of buying a plastic bag each time you go shopping.

The worst kind of waste is **SINGLE-USE PLASTIC**. Plastic cups and bottles are used once, then thrown away, but other items, like plastic basketballs, are used again and again.

TRINKETS AND TOYS

When buying (or asking for) gifts, look for something that will last, rather than break after a few uses and end up in the trash.

GREEN GIFTS

Glittery, metallic wrapping paper and ribbons can't be recycled. So save used wrapping for the next round of gift-giving. Or, even better, find alternative ways of wrapping gifts. Brightly patterned cloth works well.

Don't let birthday balloons drift into the sky – they pollute the environment when they land, and animals can choke on them.

ECO-FRIENDLY PETS

When picking a new pet, find a trusty breeder or better still adopt from a shelter. Pets have an impact on the environment too – the smaller your pet and the less meat it eats, the better. Ducks, chickens and rabbits are some of the most eco-friendly pets in the world. Chickens will provide you with fresh eggs, too!

Chickens come in all shapes and sizes. Bantams, like this one, are mini-chickens.

FAST FASHION

When clothing is mass-produced using cheap fabric, it is known as **FAST FASHION**. The items are worn a few times before fading and tearing, and soon end up in a landfill, where the cheap dyes seep into the soil. It's best to buy high-quality clothing that will last, and can be handed down to someone else when you've outgrown it.

One day, I want to start a clothing brand with cool designs, made from good material that will last a long time.

BEST BUYS

When buying something, check for tags or stickers showing where it came from. Local is best, because it means it wasn't shipped from far away, using fuels that pollute.

Remember to select food that has as little packaging as possible.

Support local farmers' markets instead of buying food imported from overseas.

CREATIVE CARDS

It's easy, and great fun, to make your own greeting cards by reusing paper, plastic, cardboard and fabric. Follow these steps to make a giraffe collage.

ASK ADULTS FOR HELP IN

cutting a cardboard base • tracing the shape of the giraffe • cutting the cardboard frame

WHAT YOU'LL NEED:
- White and brown cardboard
- Old magazines to tear up
- Yellow Pages telephone directory or newspaper
- Brown and white used cardboard or shoe boxes
- Tin foil
- Black plastic
- Tissue paper or cotton wool
- Yellow fabric or felt
- Clear paper glue
- Paint
- Black marker or koki pen
- Scissors

WHAT TO DO:
To make this giraffe card, you will need a sturdy backing, such as thick white paper or cardboard, for sticking all your bits and pieces on to when assembling your card. Leave the other side of the board blank for your message.

1. Cut strips of blue paper from old magazine pages and glue them down horizontally to create the sky. For the grass, tear strips of green magazine paper. Stick them vertically onto the lower part of the card. Don't worry if the pieces overlap.

2. To make the frame, cut several long pieces of cardboard. Each piece should be about 3cm wide. Using scissors, cut along the edges to make a wavy pattern. Glue the strips down and decorate them with shapes cut from tin foil and white cardboard.

3. For the giraffe, tear a page from an old Yellow Pages telephone directory (or newspaper) and trace the shape of the animal on the paper. Cut it out and glue it on the card.

4. Create the mane by making little cuts along one side of a rectangular piece of black plastic. Glue the uncut section to the neck. Follow the same method for the tail tuft.

5. Cut small, cardboard shapes to make the spots and glue them to the body. Colour the spots and hooves and draw the face and the horns with a black koki pen.

6. Add tree branches cut from corrugated cardboard and leaves made by scrunching up green-coloured magazine pages. Crumple white tissue wrapping paper for the clouds (cotton wool will also work) and glue a piece of yellow fabric or paper to add a bright sun.

Created by Theo van der Merwe
www.theodorvandermerweart.com

You can create all kinds of things from plastic bottles and old newspapers. I made this baobab tree! First, ask an adult to make a few holes in the bottle (later, you will poke some of your twigs through them). Place a handful of pebbles in the bottle to keep it balanced. Scrunch up newspaper into balls and fill the container about halfway. Place twigs in the top of the container, and poke some through the holes to make branches that grow sideways. Anchor the twigs with damp serviettes and liquid glue. After it has dried, paint the container. Add glitter or fairy dust and use playdough for the leaves.

WHY TREES MATTER

The health of every living thing on Earth depends on trees. These plants provide essentials such as fresh air and food, as well as countless other services: from building material and medicine to fuel and flood protection.

COCONUTS AND CASHEWS

Trees feed us by providing apples, apricots, plums, peaches, cherries, coconuts, mangoes . . . the list goes on. Walnuts, cashews and other nuts also come from trees, as do many spices, including cinnamon. Cocoa trees produce the main ingredient in chocolate. Trees also provide food for animals who eat leaves, flowers and nectar.

HOMES AND HABITATS

Hundreds of millions of people live in forests, as do countless creatures, such as chameleons, monkeys, squirrels, tree frogs, spiders, insects and birds.

Bushbabies spend most of their life in trees.

CLIMATE CONTROL

Trees protect us from extreme weather. They screen us from violent winds, filter harsh sunlight, and shield us from rain, sleet and hail. Like all living things, trees breathe (through their leaves). In doing so, they release water vapour back into the atmosphere, where it can form rain clouds and provide rain.

Fallen leaves provide a habitat for insect species in winter. They also return valuable nutrients to the soil as they decay.

FROM PULP TO PAPER

Look around you – from fences to furniture, how many things are made from wood? Paper is made by chopping wood into fine pieces, boiling it into a pulpy slush, and squeezing it into thin sheets. Without wood, we would not have musical instruments such as guitars and pianos. Wood is also a fuel used for heating, boiling water and cooking food.

A MIGHTY SHIELD

When land is worn away by forces such as wind and water, it is known as **EROSION**. Tree roots combat erosion by holding the soil in place, keeping it from being washed or blown away.

THE LUNGS OF THE PLANET

Trees make their own food using sunlight, carbon dioxide and water, a process known as **PHOTOSYNTHESIS**. So, whereas we breathe in oxygen and breathe out carbon dioxide, trees do the opposite – they soak up carbon dioxide and release oxygen.

BY ABSORBING THIS GREENHOUSE GAS, TREES CLEAN THE AIR AND COMBAT CLIMATE CHANGE.

LIVING PHARMACIES

Humans have used parts of trees to soothe aches and pains for thousands of years. Aspirin, for example, comes from the bark of willow trees. Today, scientists are still discovering new medicinal compounds in trees.

Hug a tree today! I'm happy when I'm surrounded by trees. They're a natural playground where we can climb, explore and picnic. The beautiful colours and shapes of trees have inspired many paintings, poems and songs.

FLOODS AND FILTERS

Forests protect us from floods: they absorb heavy rainfall that would otherwise flow downhill. The roots also act as a natural filter, helping to clean drinking water.

FANTASTIC FORESTS

The vast Congolian **RAINFOREST** spans six countries in Central Africa. This ancient forest is precious, because it creates a range of habitats from ground level to the canopy, which can reach as high as 50m.

Unique **MANGROVE** forests grow along seashores and riverbanks. Their dense tangles of roots slow the movement of waves and storm surges, reducing erosion and stabilising the coastline.

Technically, **BAMBOO** is not a tree but a grass. It makes for tough building material, and is a fantastic renewable resource because it grows so quickly. Some bamboo species can grow a metre each day.

Saving the planet
ONE TREE AT A TIME

In one of the driest and poorest places on the planet, a new world wonder is taking root. Dozens of countries are working together to plant a great green wall of trees to stop the desert from spreading.

WELCOME TO THE SAHEL

The Sahel is a long, narrow region at the southern edge of the Sahara Desert in Africa. Here, temperatures are rising faster than anywhere else on Earth. Farmers suffer because of severe droughts.

CREEPING DUNES

When water is scarce, plants die, and there is nothing to hold the Sahel's precious, fertile topsoil in place. It is swept away by the wind, and the dry sands of the Sahara Desert can spread even further.

MAURITANIA   MALI   NIGER
SENEGAL
BURKINA FASO
NIGERIA

THE GREAT GREEN WALL

A massive forest is emerging on the edge of the Sahara Desert. Thousands of people are doing their part to plant billions of seeds and grow millions of trees. By 2030, this Great Green Wall will be 8,000km long and will stretch across the entire width of Africa.

FIGHTING THE DESERT

The growing desert and the change in climate make it hard to live there or grow food. Millions of people go hungry and leave their homeland in search of jobs. But many African countries believe that planting trees is the first step to solving this crisis.

I sponsored a young baobab tree to be planted in Senegal. This special tree stores water in its round trunk, provides shelter, and is a source of food. Can you spot my baobab on the map? My tree might live for over a thousand years!

DESERT DATE

ACACIA

CHAD

SUDAN

ERITREA

TOUGH TREES

Only the most drought-resistant trees are being planted, such as acacia, mango and cashew. The desert date is also a good choice. It has thick bark, which protects it from bushfires.

HEALING THE LAND

By reforesting the Sahel, sand dunes are transformed into fertile land that can support crops. Trees, shrubs and grasses create habitats for insects and other animals.

MANGO

A REASON TO STAY

The Great Green Wall shows that we can work with nature, and transform an arid wasteland into a place where people can work, grow food, and live.

BAOBAB

REFORESTATION CREATES JOBS FOR PEOPLE, AND CHANGES THE LANDSCAPE SO IT CAN PRODUCE MORE FOOD.

CASHEW

ROOTS, SHOOTS AND FRUITS

Make a difference and plant your own tree in the garden or at school. Choose the new addition wisely. It is always better to select an indigenous tree – one that occurs naturally in your region.

1. DO YOUR RESEARCH

Decide which species of tree suits your environment and climate. The local garden centre or nursery can help you select a healthy tree and advise on how to take care of it. Stock up on organic fertiliser too.

2. PICK A SPOT

Find out how high and wide your tree will become. Be sure to choose a spot with enough space for a fully grown tree. Then grab a spade, and dig the hole! It must be as deep as the planting bag, and twice as wide.

Moisten the soil the night before you plant.

3. PREPARE THE SOIL

Put a few handfuls of fertiliser in the hole and mix it with some of the soil you've dug up. Then remove the plastic bag encasing the root ball, and place the tree into the centre of the hole.

Be careful not to damage the roots.

4. FEED AND WATER

Pack the soil around the root ball – compact enough to keep the stem upright. Water the tree well. Add a 5–10cm layer of mulch (leaves, stones, bark and straw) on top.

Food for rapid growth!

5. ANCHOR YOUR TREE

Plant a sturdy wooden pole or a thick branch in the soil next to your tree and tie your tree to it. This will support your tree in windy weather and make sure it grows straight.

6. KEEP TRACK

Measure your tree every six months. Who grows faster – you or the tree?

142cm

LOPPERS, POPPERS AND CHOPPERS

Sometimes, the best thing you can do for an ecosystem is to remove the plants that don't belong there. These invaders or 'aliens' can drive indigenous species to extinction.

1. UNDERSTAND THE ISSUE

When non-indigenous species enter an ecosystem (whether on purpose or by accident), they risk becoming invasive. They have no natural enemies and spread aggressively, disturbing the natural balance.

This beautiful plant is a poisonous invader. It is known as the mother-of-millions because it spreads so rapidly.

2. KNOW YOUR WEEDS

Weeds are plants that grow where they aren't wanted. They endanger ecosystems by consuming too much water, releasing chemicals into the soil, and displacing native species. This affects animals too.

South Africans imported water hyacinths from the Amazon as decorative pond flowers. But the plant has spread wildly, and is now clogging its rivers and dams.

3. SPOT THE SPECIES

Certain invasive species are such a big threat that they must be removed by law. Your local botanical garden can tell you what the problem species in your area are. Keep an eye out, and report the aliens!

Have you seen the invasive pompom weed?

4. JOIN A HACK

To stop the spread of alien species, people hack them out with axes, saws, poppers, loppers, clippers and other tools. The more hands available to pull tiny seedlings from the ground, the better.

Poppers rip trees out – roots and all

OTHER INVADERS

All kinds of organisms can become invasive, such as exotic pet snakes set free by their owners, starfish and crabs clinging to ship hulls as they travel to new waters, and rats stowing away on trains, boats and trucks.

As instinctive predators, **HOUSE CATS** are one of the worst invasive species. When five pet cats were brought to Marion Island in 1949, they reproduced quickly, to more than 3,000 in 25 years, and killed countless defenceless nesting seabirds.

Cute, but deadly! Cats are born hunters.

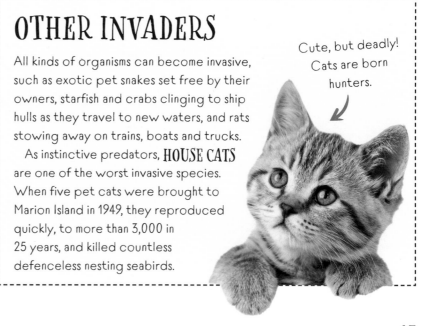

EVERY LAST DROP

Fresh water is a precious resource, especially in Africa, where droughts are common and many water sources, such as rivers, are polluted. Only half of South African families have clean, fresh water piped into their homes. Luckily, many charities are building wells, dams and water filters to help people without access to clean drinking water. Do your part to save water by following these ten tips at home.

TURN OFF THE TAP. Don't leave the water running while you are brushing your teeth. And when washing the dishes, rather fill a basin instead of washing under running water.

REUSE YOUR TOWELS. Don't drop your bath towel in the laundry basket after each use (you're clean when you use it!). Hang it out to dry and use it for a few days in a row.

DON'T RUSH TO FLUSH. It varies from toilet to toilet, but one flush can use as much as 11 litres of water! Don't waste flushes on used tissues – drop them in the trash.

USE IT TWICE. Catch water in a bucket while you shower and scoop out used bath water. It can be used to flush toilet bowls or to water the garden (if not too soapy).

LISTEN FOR DRIPS. Catch rainwater runoff in buckets, and use it in the garden. Keep an ear out for drips – find all those leaking taps, hoses and faucets, and have them fixed.

DON'T OVERFILL THE POOL. If it's very full, water splashes out easily. Also, get a pool cover – it keeps the water from evaporating (turning from liquid to vapour in the heat of the sun).

PLANT A WATERWISE GARDEN. Choose succulents, which are hardy and perfectly suited to dry conditions. They come in all sorts of interesting shapes, sizes and colours.

CHOOSE THE RIGHT TIME. It's best to water plants in the early morning or late afternoon when the sun is less fierce. In the hotter hours water is more likely to evaporate.

WASH WISELY. When cleaning a bicycle, use a bucket instead of a hose, which leads to waste. Wash your dog on the driest patch of the lawn, so that the grass is watered too.

RINSE FRUIT IN A BOWL. Don't run the tap every time you need to rinse fruit. Wash them all in the same bowl, then pour the water on indoor or outdoor plants.

The Zambezi River flows between Zimbabwe and Zambia and tumbles over the Victoria Falls (locally known as Mosi-oa-Tunya), which is more than 1,700m wide, and one of the Seven Natural Wonders of the World. Tens of millions of people rely on this river for drinking water.

FROM RAINDROP TO TAP WATER

Tap water comes from rivers and dams. It is filtered and cleaned at special treatment centres before it is piped to our homes. Nature has its own way of cleaning water. As rainwater flows through layers of rock and sand, dirt and debris get stuck and are left behind. Wetlands and swamps are fantastic natural filters. They trap dirt and absorb pollutants.

MAKE A FILTER

WHAT YOU'LL NEED:

- Large plastic bottle
- Cotton-wool balls
- Paper towels
- Cloth, such as a dish towel
- Sand (coarse and/or fine)
- Gravel
- Dirty water. Make a messy mixture adding mud, bits of leaves, glitter, cooking oil, coffee grounds or crumbs to the water.

WHAT TO DO:

1. Cut off the bottom of the bottle.
2. Stuff cotton balls into the bottle-neck. Wedge them in tightly!
3. Add a layer of folded paper towels over the cotton balls.
4. Add a layer of crumpled cloth.
5. Add clean sand: first the fine sand, then the coarse sand on top.
6. The gravel is your final top layer.
7. Balance your filter on a glass jar (to catch the water passing through).
8. Pour dirty water into the filter, and wait to see the clean(er) water drip out at the bottom.

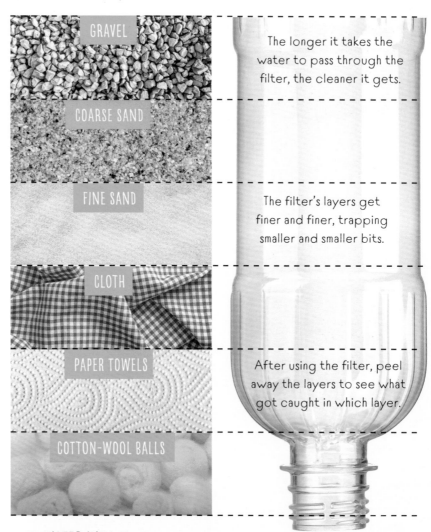

GRAVEL

COARSE SAND

FINE SAND

CLOTH

PAPER TOWELS

COTTON-WOOL BALLS

The longer it takes the water to pass through the filter, the cleaner it gets.

The filter's layers get finer and finer, trapping smaller and smaller bits.

After using the filter, peel away the layers to see what got caught in which layer.

YOUR WATER WILL BE MUCH CLEANER – BUT IT IS NOT SAFE TO DRINK! USE IT IN THE GARDEN OR ON INDOOR PLANTS INSTEAD.

ETHICAL EATING

Everything on the supermarket shelf has a carbon footprint. How big a footprint depends on how much land was used to produce it, whether greenhouse gases were released, and how far it had to travel from farm to fork.

A lot of leftovers end up in landfills. Avoid wasting food: Don't pile more on your plate than you can eat • Don't be picky about fruits that have a few spots • Check the 'Best by' date and use ingredients before they expire • Freeze big meals instead of leaving them to go mouldy in the fridge • Place your scraps on the compost heap (see page 53!)

MEAT OR VEGGIES?

Of all the meals in the world, beef has the biggest carbon footprint. It takes a lot of resources to raise and farm cattle. Cows also fart and burp the greenhouse gas methane, directly contributing to climate change. Try to swop some red meat meals for more eco-friendly nuts, fruit and vegetables.

PICK YOUR FISH

The South African Sustainable Seafood Initiative, or SASSI, helps people make responsible choices when ordering seafood. Each species on the menu is classified as green, orange or red (like a traffic light). Green fish are the most sustainable – they have big populations and are caught by more eco-friendly fishing methods. Think twice before ordering orange species – they are under pressure from overfishing. Red species are a hard no. Ask a parent to download the SASSI app if you're eating fish tonight.

When getting takeaways, say no to extra packaging, serviettes and single-use knives and forks.

Fruits such as oranges, tangerines and blueberries are harvested at a specific time of year. The rest of the time they are imported from elsewhere in the world. Minimise the impact of shipping by eating only fruit that is in season.

BAKE YOUR OWN BUNS

Instead of buying from the store, follow the recipe below to make your own burger buns or hotdog rolls. This soft bread has a golden colour, chewy texture and rich taste.

INGREDIENTS (FOR 8 BUNS)

- 240g of warm water
- 3 tbsp (45ml) milk
- 1 packet of instant dry yeast
- 2 tbsp (30ml) sugar
- 465g flour
- 1 tbsp (15ml) salt
- 35g butter, softened at room temperature
- 2 eggs, beaten lightly
- Sesame seeds (optional, to sprinkle on top)

PREP: Line a baking sheet with non-stick baking paper.

- Combine the warm water, milk, yeast and sugar, and leave the mixture to stand for 5 minutes.
- Sift flour and salt together in mixing bowl.
- Add the softened butter to the mix and mix lightly with your fingers until the mixture resembles fresh breadcrumbs.
- Make an indent in the flour mix. Stir in the yeast liquid and then add the beaten eggs.
- Knead the dough for 8–10 minutes by hand until it feels smooth and elastic. (Alternatively, you can knead it for 5–8 minutes in an electric mixer with the dough hook attachment.) Kneading is an important step – it combines the ingredients and helps to 'wake up' the yeast, develop the gluten and incorporate air into the dough, making it strong enough to rise and not fall flat.
- Shape the dough into a big ball. Place it in a lightly greased bowl and cover loosely with a clean dish towel. Leave it to stand in a warmish place for 1–2 hours until it has risen nicely. It should almost double in size.
- Divide the dough into eight equal parts.
- Gently form the pieces into round burger buns or long hotdog rolls.

- Arrange the rolls 5–7cm apart on the baking sheet and cover loosely with the dish towel.
- Leave the rolls to rise again, for 1–2 hours.
- Preheat the oven to 200°C, and position the oven rack in the centre of the oven.
- Beat an egg together with a little water. Brush the risen rolls with the egg and sprinkle with sesame seeds.
- Place the loaded tray into the oven and bake for ± 15 minutes. Halfway through the baking time, turn the baking sheet around. The rolls should be golden brown when done. Cool before eating.

FINAL PRODUCT!

51

IN THE GARDEN

Time to dig in the dirt! Starting a vegetable garden, even a small one, is a fun way to spend time outside, to connect with the earth and to grow your own food.

PLANTING POTATOES

Potatoes have 'eyes' – that is, small knobs where a stem will sprout from. You can buy special 'seed potatoes' that already have well-developed eyes, or hunt for knobby potatoes at the store.

To prepare potatoes for planting, place them in an old egg carton on a sunny windowsill, with the eyes facing up. When the eyes have sprouted little stems of 1–2cm (usually after about ten days) the potatoes are ready to go in the ground! Plant them 10cm deep, 20cm apart, and with the sprouting stems facing up. They'll be ready to harvest within about three months.

GROW SEEDLINGS IN EGGSHELL POTS

WHAT YOU'LL NEED:
- Egg cartons and eggs
- Pre-moistened seed-starting mix
- Seeds (herbs and small plants work best in these tiny 'egg pots')

WHAT TO DO:
1. Crack the eggs in half (uneven breaks are fine).
2. Rinse the shells well.
3. Fill the halves with soil.
4. Plant a seed or two in each.
5. Put the 'egg pots' in the carton, and place it somewhere sunny.
6. Add a few drops of water every couple of days to keep the soil moist but not soaked.
7. When the seedlings are over 5cm tall, move them to a bigger pot or garden bed. Gently crush the bottom of the egg shell and plant the whole thing, shards and all.

The eggshell will decay as the plant grows, providing valuable nutrients, such as calcium.

You don't need a big backyard to start a vegetable garden. You can use pots on a windowsill or balcony, a hanging basket, or a trellis against a sunny wall. Visit your local gardening centre to find out how much room and what kind of care different vegetables require.

Gardeners love earthworms. These soft, slimy animals till the earth as they tunnel and feed, swallowing mouthfuls of soil that contain delicious scraps of plants, fungi and manure. Earthworms break down waste and recycle nutrients. Their tunnels help the ground to absorb more water.

I started my own veggie garden in the backyard! My tasty cherry tomatoes were ready for harvest after 50 days. My carrots are almost ready. I recently planted okra seeds. Okra is nutritious and yummy.

DO'S AND DON'TS FOR YOUR COMPOST HEAP

Organic waste can be **COMPOSTED**, meaning that it is broken down to make useful fertiliser for the garden. Not all organic waste should go onto the compost heap, however – some organic matter creates bad smells, breeds bacteria and attracs pests. Note what can and can't be composted at home.

- Fruit and vegetables
- Bread, rolls and crumbs
- Ketchup, mustard and other condiments
- Mouldy jam
- Nutshells
- Leaves and grasses

- Meat, fat and bones
- Milk and cheese
- Seafood
- Dog and cat poop
- Oils or greasy foods
- Plants that have been sprayed with pesticide

DAYS FØR ACTION

Mark your calendar! There are dozens of special environmental days every year. Here are a few favourites — but if you do your own research, you'll find many more.

DO SOMETHING SPECIAL!

Here are some cool classroom activities to celebrate these important days:

- Write a story • Wear a costume
- Do a show-and-tell • Make a poster
- Invite a speaker • Put on a play
- Draw a picture • Invent a game

ARBOR WEEK
1-7 SEPTEMBER
(IN SOUTH AFRICA)

From Canada to Cuba, Australia to Venezuela – countries all over the world have tree-planting days. The best time to plant a seedling differs from place to place: people in Poland prefer October, while Ugandans plant their trees in March. Join the global movement – plant your own!

DARK SKY WEEK
THE NEW MOON IN APRIL

Light pollution blots the stars from our view. During Dark Sky Week, people worldwide switch their lights off early so that we can view our galaxy in greater detail.

WORLD OCEANS DAY
8 JUNE

As far as scientists know, Earth is the only planet with oceans. Its waters teem with life: from free-floating plankton smaller than the dot on this i, to the blue whale, the largest animal on the planet. Celebrate World Oceans Day by learning something new about this remarkable underwater world: head to the library, watch a marine-themed documentary or visit an aquarium.

POLAR BEAR DAY
27 FEBRUARY

The thick-furred polar bear roams the icy Arctic landscape, led by its incredible nose. It can smell its seal prey over 30km away. Polar bears are threatened by climate change: rising temperatures melt the ice, shrinking their habitat.

WORLD ORCA DAY
14 JULY

Orcas are beautiful, highly intelligent dolphins. They are often called 'wolves of the ocean' because they hunt in packs (called pods). Pods are led by the oldest female. These incredible predators hunt prey as large as sharks and whales.

ANIMAL EVENTS

SEA TURTLE DAY
16 JUNE

FROG DAY
20 MARCH

CHEETAH DAY
4 DECEMBER

SLOTH DAY
20 OCTOBER

PARROT DAY
31 MAY

BAT APPRECIATION DAY
17 APRIL

Bats may look a bit creepy, but they pollinate plants, spread seeds, and keep insects away from farmers' crops. Stand up for these misunderstood mammals — they make the world a better place.

CLEAN-UP DAY
THIRD SUNDAY OF SEPTEMBER

Time to organise a clean-up, whether it's at the park, beach, river or the fence around your school where scraps of plastic get stuck.

Romario's guide to being an
ECO-WARRIOR

PICK A CAUSE

WHAT'S YOUR PASSION? LEARN ALL YOU CAN ABOUT YOUR CHOSEN CAUSE.

SET A GOAL

Decide how you would like to help. It's best to start small. Simple goals like 'I want to save water at home' or 'I want to write a story to inspire others' will already make a difference! Big goals, such as 'I want to raise money for charity' can be more achievable if broken into small steps.

JOIN FORCES!

Find your people! After-school clubs are great for meeting friends that share your interests. They might include tree planters, insect lovers, aquarium fans and recycling champions.

USE YOUR TALENTS

We all have different strengths. Maybe you're good with animals, or a creative poster designer, or a poet who can write inspiring tunes. Use your talents, and have fun doing your bit to help the Earth.

Are you a future chef? Host a bake sale and raise funds for a worthy cause!

SPEAK UP!

A powerful speech can inspire others to join your cause. Make sure you speak in a tone you're comfortable with – it doesn't have to be stiff and formal. Use attention-grabbing facts, and keep your talk short and punchy.

Public speaking is not for everyone. You can spark a change by writing letters to politicians, asking newspapers and magazines to cover an issue, or by posting online.

STAY SAFE! It's best to have a parent run your social media account.

TAKING ACTION

FUNDRAISING

Pick a charity close to your heart, and donate to it by hosting a: bake sale • sponsored fun run • online crowdfunding campaign • dress-up day at school • raffle • second-hand pop-up shop

VOLUNTEERING

Volunteers spend their free time helping others. Join a fun day out, be it planting veggies at a community garden, hunting for nurdles on the beach, or hacking out invasive plants.

COUNTING

Environmental groups are always looking for sharp eyes to help count endangered birds and plants. Join a census walk! They collect valuable information and use it to make decisions about conservation.

KEEP SMILING! Your goals might feel far away, but stay positive. Baby steps become big leaps!

MY FUTURE

Interested in a career as an eco-warrior? Do this quiz to find out which environmental field suits you. Pick one reply per question.

Which describes you best?
A. I'd rather spend time with other people than be by myself
B. I like working with my hands
C. I can entertain myself with my own imagination
D. I get along better with animals than with people

What kind of student are you?
A. I take detailed notes
B. I prefer practical sessions
C. I doodle in the margins
D. I enjoy doing my own research

You're doing a group project on endangered birds for school. Which task is yours?
A. I present the final product to the class and teacher – public speaking comes easily
B. I come up with a design for nesting platforms – I enjoy solving problems and making plans
C. I find cool pictures and illustrate the cover – I am creative and have an eye for striking design
D. I research the habits and habitats of endangered birds – I like learning about nature and what we can do to conserve it

It's dress-up day, and you have four costumes to pick from. Which one do you chose?
A. Judge with a big curly wig
B. Giant LEGO block
C. Rockstar with a guitar
D. Scuba diver

Which after-school club would you most like to join?
A. Debating
B. Robotics
C. Photography
D. Hiking

What are your favourite kinds of books to read?
A. Historical fiction
B. Computer guides
C. Graphic novels
D. Adventure novels

If you had to pick your homework, which would it be?
A. Preparing a speech
B. Doing a construction project
C. Writing an essay
D. Researching an interesting topic

Where would you most like to volunteer?
A. Charity fundraisers, such as selling raffle tickets or hosting a quiz
B. Building shelters at a wildlife sanctuary
C. Designing flyers or punchy posters to raise awareness
D. Cleaning penguins after an oil spill

What videos do you like watching when you're online?
A. News
B. People playing computer games
C. How-to-draw tutorials
D. Mini-documentaries

It's the weekend! How do you spend Saturday morning?
A. Arguing with a sibling over which TV channel to watch
B. Building a car with toothpicks and bottle caps
C. Reading a book – or writing my own
D. Teaching my pet a new trick

My favourite outing is to a:
A. Museum
B. Science centre
C. Art gallery
D. Game reserve

MOSTLY As – POLITICS AND LAW

Politicians are elected to represent their community in parliament, where important decisions are made. They can propose policies and laws to stop overfishing, ban certain plastics and reduce the emission of greenhouse gases, for example. Environmental lawyers deal with legal issues, such as water laws and land management, and can keep big businesses from over-exploiting natural resources and polluting the environment.

MOSTLY Bs – ENGINEERING AND INVENTING

Engineers are problem solvers who enjoy tinkering with technology. They design and build a wide variety of machines and structures – from wind turbines and solar panels to hydro-electricity plants that can replace coal-powered stations. They can design dams and plan sustainable cities. Engineers work to improve old systems to use natural resources more efficiently. They also come up with new, eco-friendly inventions.

MOSTLY Cs – ARTS AND MEDIA

People working in the media, such as journalists, photographers and vloggers, communicate information to the public, and also educate and entertain. Authors, filmmakers and even songwriters spark change with their craft. Some write catchy conservation slogans or drive awareness campaigns. Artists can illustrate scientific textbooks – or create beautiful abstract art to draw attention to issues that they feel strongly about.

MOSTLY Ds – ECOLOGY AND ZOOLOGY

Scientists who study plants, animals and the environment have a passion for the natural world. Ecologists focus on the relationships between living things (including humans) and their environment. Botanists study plants. Zoologists study animals, and some become specialists – ornithologists study birds, for example, while herpetologists research reptiles and amphibians, and entomologists study insects.

GLOSSARY

ACTIVIST

Someone who fights for a cause (such as wildlife conservation or world peace) and works to bring about change.

ATMOSPHERE

The mixture of gases surrounding our planet; also known as air.

BIODIVERSITY

The variety of life, including plants, animals, insects, fungi and microscopic creatures in a particular habitat.

CARBON

A chemical element found in all living things. It combines with other elements to form compounds such as carbon dioxide, which is a greenhouse gas.

CARBON FOOTPRINT

The amount of carbon dioxide someone releases into the environment, usually measured over a year.

CLIMATE

The typical weather conditions of a place, measured over many years. In contrast, 'weather' is measured over a short time – such as a windy morning or a chilly night.

DEFORESTATION

Cutting down trees or whole forests for firewood, furniture and paper, or to make room for farms or buildings.

DESERTIFICATION

The spread of a desert. Many things can cause desertification to happen, such as drought, fires, overgrazing and deforestation.

E-WASTE

Electronic waste, such as old smartphones, laptops and tablets.

ECO-FRIENDLY

Something that doesn't harm the environment.

ENDANGERED

At risk of dying out.

EROSION

The wearing away of rocks and soil by forces such as wind, water and ice.

EXTINCTION

When all members of a species are dead. If a species is categorised as 'Extinct in the wild', it means that some living members are kept in captivity (in zoos, for example).

FOSSIL FUELS

Fuels such as coal, oil and natural gas that formed from the remains of animals and plants that died millions of years ago and are buried deep below ground.

GLOBAL WARMING

The gradual rising of the Earth's atmospheric temperature.

WORD SEARCH: FIND THE GLOSSARY TERMS

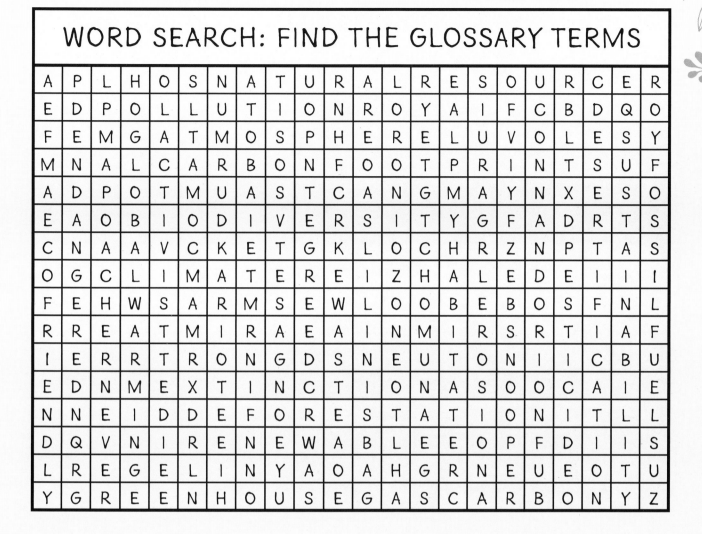

A	P	L	H	O	S	N	A	T	U	R	A	L	R	E	S	O	U	R	C	E	R
E	D	P	O	L	L	U	T	I	O	N	R	O	Y	A	I	F	C	B	D	Q	O
F	E	M	G	A	T	M	O	S	P	H	E	R	E	L	U	V	O	L	E	S	Y
M	N	A	L	C	A	R	B	O	N	F	O	O	T	P	R	I	N	T	S	U	F
A	D	P	O	T	M	U	A	S	T	C	A	N	G	M	A	Y	N	X	E	S	O
E	A	O	B	I	O	D	I	V	E	R	S	I	T	Y	G	F	A	D	R	T	S
C	N	A	A	V	C	K	E	T	G	K	L	O	C	H	R	Z	N	P	T	A	S
O	G	C	L	I	M	A	T	E	R	E	I	Z	H	A	L	E	D	E	I	I	I
F	E	H	W	S	A	R	M	S	E	W	L	O	O	B	E	B	O	S	F	N	L
R	R	E	A	T	M	I	R	A	E	A	I	N	M	I	R	S	R	T	I	A	F
I	E	R	R	T	R	O	N	G	D	S	N	E	U	T	O	N	I	I	C	B	U
E	D	N	M	E	X	T	I	N	C	T	I	O	N	A	S	O	O	C	A	I	E
N	N	E	I	D	D	E	F	O	R	E	S	T	A	T	I	O	N	I	T	L	L
D	Q	V	N	I	R	E	N	E	W	A	B	L	E	E	O	P	F	D	I	I	S
L	R	E	G	E	L	I	N	Y	A	O	A	H	G	R	N	E	U	E	O	T	U
Y	G	R	E	E	N	H	O	U	S	E	G	A	S	C	A	R	B	O	N	Y	Z

GREENHOUSE GAS
A heat-trapping gas, such as methane.

HABITAT
The natural home of a particular species.

NATURAL RESOURCE
Something useful found in nature.

OZONE
A layer of gas that protects life on Earth by absorbing the sun's harmful ultraviolet rays.

PESTICIDE
A poisonous chemical mix used to kill creatures that are considered to be pests.

POACHER
Someone who illegally captures or kills wild animals, or removes and sells rare plants.

POLLUTION
The introduction of something harmful into the environment.

RENEWABLE
Referring to a resource that doesn't run out when used, such as sunlight.

SUSTAINABILITY
Using resources responsibly, so that there will be enough left for future generations.

PICTURE CREDITS

GOODBYE FOR NOW!

Since doing my first beach clean-up at age six, my environmental journey has led me to many wonderful people around the world. They all share the same vision: to protect our home, Earth. I want to thank everyone who has supported me so far, especially my parents, who always believe in me.

MY FIRST CLEAN-UP

I hope to remain happy in my heart, to continue being an Earth Guardian, and to help others along this path. I believe optimism, kindness and action can save the world.

We can create a better, sustainable future by planting trees, protecting habitats, recycling . . . and by following the other eco-friendly lifestyle tips you've just read about!

I hope my book motivates other aspiring eco-warriors. Let's find innovative ways to protect our beautiful planet and its biodiversity. You too can make a positive change. Keep smiling and be a visionary!

Interior Design
Inspirations
FROM COTTAGES TO CASTLES

Editor | Publisher Janet Verdeguer
Photography by Barry Grossman,
Craig Denis and Naim Chidiac

Perla Lichi

Interior Design Inspirations
From Cottages to Castles
Copyright © 2017 by Perla Lichi

Library of Congress Control Number: 2017900119

ISBN 978-0-9889910-7-1
Published by Granny Apple Publishing LLC
Sarasota, FL USA 34241

Copyright © 2017 by Perla Lichi
Printed in China by
Four Color Print Group, Louisville, KY

A c k n o w l e d g m e n t s

Inspirations is my sixth book and I am especially pleased that it presents the full range of my work—from the decorating of a newlywed couple's first one-bedroom apartment to some of the most grand and exotic palaces around the world that I have been honored to design.

This incredible work does not happen by accident, nor do I accomplish it single handedly. I want to thank my hard-working and talented team, which altogether represents individuals from 22 different nationalities. Through their enthusiasm, experience and skills, each project comes to life. They are always there to help me turn my design concepts into reality.

I also want to thank the many vendors, suppliers and craftspeople whose work has contributed to all of my interior design projects—including these cottages and castles. Through their unique talents and products, they help us keep abreast of the latest materials, technology and innovations that enable us to pull everything together for our clients.

Last but not least, I want to thank all of my clients, who believed in me and gave me artistic freedom to create their timeless cottages and castles.

~ Perla Lichi

"If you have built castles in the air, your work need
not be lost; that is where they should be.
Now put the foundations under them."
~ Henry David Thoreau

Contents

Contents

Newlyweds Cottage

Photography by Craig Denis

Newlyweds Cottage was designed for a just-married young couple starting out on their own. Like a brand new marriage, our "Newlyweds's Cottage" was designed with a light, fresh attitude of love, hope, and new beginnings. A palette of turquoise and white—almost universally appealing to both sexes—was chosen.

The continuity and easy flow between the rooms of this small, open floor plan, apartment is assured with this "safe" color combination. The geometric pattern in the living room area rug, for example, is mimicked in the master bedroom bedspread.

We believe in wall décor to add spirit and personality to a home. In this case, it's a combination of art and accessories—some of each spouse's memories and collectibles, newly purchased items, and the wedding gifts the young couple adore, but simply can't figure out what else to do with!

These interiors are infused with fun: an aqua leather swivel chair; a circular glass coffee table with a contemporary silver metallic base. In the living room all this is anchored with a conservative grey upholstered sofa that seems to say, "Look honey, we're home."

To keep your marriage brimming,
With love in the loving cup,
Whenever you're wrong, admit it;
Whenever you'right, shut up.
~ Ogden Nash

A CONSERVATIVE
UPHOLSTERED
GREY SOFA SEEMS
TO SAY "HONEY,
I'M HOME."

15

WALL DÉCOR ADDS SPIRIT AND PERSONALITY TO A HOME: A COMBINATION OF ART AND ACCESSORIES — SOME OF EACH SPOUSE'S MEMO- RIES AND MAYBE EVEN SOME WEDDING GIFTS.

City Cottage

Photography by Craig Denis

A white background is accented with furniture and accessories in today's popular peacock colors in this three-bedroom, two-and-a-half bath Miami townhouse. Because the location is Miami, the very light, reflective materials that were specified all work together to create a light, fresh look. Wall trim—white lacquer moldings with mirror inserts—visually opens up the living room and, through reflection, gives it added depth and a more spacious feeling.

We took an empty upstairs hallway and converted it into a den that we call "the loft" by adding a lower level to the existing stairway ledge that now serves as a desk. Downstairs, we created a special low divider that does double duty as a sculptural piece of art when viewed from the living room and adds an eat-in dining area in the kitchen.

Without adding a wall, we created two rooms from one. A mirror on the kitchen wall makes the space appear about three times as large as it actually is. White lacquer kitchen cabinets with horizontal pulls are accented with a grey-and-white backsplash. A trio of contemporary pendants lights up the island work area that features bar seating.

The children's rooms are especially small and placement of the windows made designing them even more difficult. Each room is decorated around a "theme." By creating custom beds positioned flush against the wall with cubby headboards, we were able to really open up these small spaces.

"A city is a place where there is no need to wait for next week to get the answer to a question, to taste the food of any country, to find new voices to listen to and familiar ones to listen to again."

~ **Margaret Mead**

MODERN
MIAMI-STYLE
AMBIANCE
WITH A WHITE
BACKGROUND
AND PEACOCK
COLORS.

21

"THE BEST AND
MOST BEAUTIFUL
THINGS IN THE
WORLD CANNOT
BE SEEN OR EVEN
TOUCHED — THEY
MUST BE FELT
WITH THE HEART."
~HELEN KELLER

AN EMPTY UPSTAIRS
HALLWAY WAS CON-
VERTED INTO A DEN
THAT WE CALL "THE
LOFT." THE KIDS' ROOMS
CALLED FOR CUSTOM
BEDS, FLUSH AGAINST
THE WALL, WITH CUBBY
HEADBOARDS.

IN THE MASTER
BEDROOM, LEMON
YELLOW WAS ADDED
TO COMPLEMENT
THE PEACOCK COLOR
SCHEME.

Bachelor Pad

Photography by Craig Denis

How many guys do you know who either have custody every other weekend, or are entirely raising a child on their own? We created a bachelor pad for such a client recently. He wanted his apartment to have a sophisticated look, but still be light and welcoming for those days when his son stays over.

Light grey walls and dark grey-and-white furniture were selected to create the background for this dual lifestyle. Decorative accessories, mostly in blue, were added for visual interest. Silver metallic and dark wood furniture, picture and mirror frames blend smoothly with the overall scheme. An eye-catching display of 66 small framed mirrors highlights the dining room feature wall. A rectangular glass dining table is positioned under a pair of matching contemporary light fixtures.

The living room seating arrangement is created with a grey leather sectional sofa around a square white pearl coffee table. The shaggy area rug features a grey-and-white geometric pattern.

A guest room is fitted out for the son, who at the moment loves anything to do with cars. Dad wanted him to always have fun and feel welcome. We advised our client that this room could change over time, as his son grows up and develops other interests. The result is a home that provides a contemporary pad for Dad when he is alone or entertaining adult guests, with a welcoming ambiance for both Dad and Son.

"Bachelors know more about women than married men;
if they didn't, they'd be married too."
~ **H. L. Mencken**

"EVEN IF YOU'RE ON
THE RIGHT TRACK,
YOU'LL GET RUN
OVER IF YOU JUST SIT
THERE."
~ WILL ROGERS

LIGHT GREY WALLS
AND DARK GREY-
AND-WHITE FURNITURE
WERE SELECTED TO
CREATE THE BACK-
GROUND FOR THIS
BACHELOR PAD.

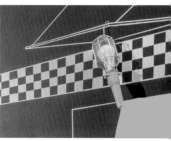

A GUEST ROOM IS
FITTED OUT FOR THE
SON, WHO AT THE
MOMENT LOVES
ANYTHING TO DO
WITH CARS.

Coastal Cottage

Photography by Craig Denis

Coastal Cottage, a one-story home with an open floor plan, features fresh styling that perfectly captures a relaxed, 21st century ambiance. We combined whites and ivories with accents of blue. The Coastal Chic look is especially adaptable to an open floor plan where the rooms all need to work together without being monotonous or boring. To create a smooth traffic flow in the living room without closing the space, we positioned a U-shaped seating area over an area rug. Artwork throughout follows the Coastal Chic theme with beachy motifs of seashells, sea birds, and coral. These are fun accessories to shop for and help you personalize your adaptation of this theme.

The kitchen, the heart of this home, is part of the family room. Two-tone cabinets with randomly spaced beaded glass doors make the cabinetry look more like furniture. Light woods and semi-gloss finishes blend well with the overall ambiance in this relaxed, comfortable open kitchen. Adjacent to the kitchen, a cozy breakfast room features tropical-style furniture, a shell-motif chandelier and coastal artwork.

In the master bedroom, linen curtains keep the look light and fresh and contrast with the engineered walnut floor that is easy to maintain and will not fade in the sunlight. The odd-shaped windows and the odd placement of windows in different sizes was a challenge that we solved by designing two-tone side panels attached to the crown molding. By placing the panels not over the windows, but in between, we created a unified bay window effect. A floor-to-ceiling custom padded headboard improves acoustics for a peaceful night's sleep. This headboard also pulls the eye upward to give the illusion that the room has higher ceilings!

"The sea does not reward those who are too anxious, too greedy, or too impatient. One should lie empty, open, choiceless as a beach— waiting for a gift from the sea."
~ **Anne Morrow Lindbergh**

BLUES, WHITES AND
IVORIES IN FABRICS AND
ACCENTS COMBINE TO
CREATE THE COASTAL
CHIC LOOK, ESPECIALLY
ADAPTABLE TO AN OPEN
FLOOR PLAN.

"ONCE YOU MAKE A
DECISION, THE UNIVERSE
CONSPIRES TO MAKE IT
HAPPEN."
~ RALPH WALDO EMERSON

49

ACCESSORIES ARE FUN TO
SHOP FOR AND WILL HELP
PERSONALIZE YOUR
ADAPTATION OF THIS
THEME.

Cozy Cottage
Photography by Barry Grossman

The clients wanted a rich, formal look that was at once comfortable and easy to care for. Because we were dealing with low ceilings, the old, flat popcorn ceiling was removed and replaced with Venetian-style, faux stone ceiling trim surrounding antique silver leaf insets. When light reflects the silver leafing, it gives the illusion of higher ceilings and crowns the room with a beautiful ceiling design. We also added dimmers to all the lights and added some new decorative lighting.

We camouflaged the ceiling vents by creating Venetian-style faux stone vent covers that coordinate with the Venetian moldings and filled in the rest with reflective silver leaf. Because the rooms in the home are square and without visual interest, arched wall panels filled with pattern and texture break up the visual monotony and give the look of a Venetian piazza.

With a click of the remote control, the flat screen TV changes from a TV into a beautifully framed piece of art above the buffet. Now one room serves two functions—living room and family room. In the arches flanking the TV, we inserted damask wallpaper and padding and placed sconces top center. In adjacent arches, we inserted tufted fabric, literally upholstery for the walls for acoustical and aesthetic benefit.

"So love is rest? The cozy corner? The little nook?
Sometimes it ought to be. Sometimes it is."
~ **Doris Lessing**

WE CAMOUFLAGED CEILING VENTS BY CREATING VENETIAN STYLE FAUX STONE VENT COVERS THAT COORDINATE WITH THE VENETIAN MOLDING.

Villa Sorrento

Photography by Craig Denis

This is a 4,000-square-foot home with five bedrooms plus loft/study and three bathrooms. Marble-like Italian porcelain flooring was installed through the main living areas. A custom, marble, waterjet medallion and border creates the ambiance of a grand entryway.

Custom gold accents were added to existing wrought iron stair railings. In the living room, new custom furniture was arranged over an area rug. Faux finishes and applied moldings with wallpaper inserts were used to enhance and create architectural detailing on ceilings, walls, and arched entryways.

In the dining room, a custom bar area with a dark marble top was added in an existing niche and highlighted with mirrors, lighting and wooden shelves with glass inserts. A dining table with marquetry top and gold accents is surrounded by custom upholstered dining chairs. In the master bedroom, a custom headboard wall with silk velvet upholstered panels is enhanced with crystal buttons. Carvings in the woodwork are highlighted with silver leaf finish. An etched glass panel in gold and silver leaf was installed over existing windows by the tub area of the master bath.

And you say: "I am leaving, goodbye."
You go away from my heart,
away from the land of love,
And you have the heart not to come back.

But please do not go away,
do not give me this pain.
Come back to Sorrento,
let me live!

~ Neapolitan song composed in 1902 by Ernesto De Curtis;
words by his brother, the poet and painter Giambattista De Curtis.

THE DINING TABLE,
WITH MARQUETRY TOP
AND GOLD ACCENTS, IS
SURROUNDED BY CUSTOM
UPHOLSTERED DINING
CHAIRS.

69

CUSTOM GOLD ACCENTS
WERE ADDED TO
EXISTING WROUGHT
IRON STAIR RAILINGS.

THE CUSTOM HEADBOARD
WALL, WITH SILK VELVET
UPHOLSTERED PANELS, IS
ENHANCED WITH
BUTTONS OF CRYSTAL.
CARVINGS IN THE WOOD-
WORK ARE HIGHLIGHTED
WITH SILVER LEAF.

Villa Moderne

Photography by Craig Denis

Located on the water in an old Miami neighborhood, surrounded by lush, tropical foliage and a lot of natural sunlight, this home called for a very light, airy, fresh décor. The client entertains frequently and wanted a sophisticated, contemporary look with a touch of bling. The client's artwork was to be used as a focal point but they did not want the colors in the artwork to carry through our design.

We absolutely bedazzled the living room fireplace — and our clients — with silver and crystal and white onyx! Dual seating areas were anchored with back-to-back sofas and positioned as a center island over the area rug. Traffic flows 360 degrees around this dual seating area, making it easy to get to the family room, the dining room and the office.

A custom sculptural white lacquer dining table features mirror inserts that reflect the antique silver leaf ceiling and crystal chandelier. The dining room ceiling appears higher than it actually is through the use of three decorating techniques: silver leafing, lighting, and reflection.

Champagne velvet damask with metallic silver embossing enhances the dining chairs. It was designed and fabricated in Turkey specifically for this project. The neutral color scheme flows perfectly from the living room into the dining room. Classic crown molding in both rooms was finished in high gloss lacquer and adorned with silver leafing for a crisp, modern look.

"Simplicity is about subtracting the obvious and adding the meaningful."

~ John Maeda, TheLaws of Simplicity:

Design, Technology, Business, Life

THE CLIENT'S ARTWORK
WAS TO BE USED AS A
FOCAL POINT BUT THEY
DID NOT WANT THE
COLORS IN THE ARTWORK
TO CARRY THROUGH OUR
DESIGN.

81

WE MADE THE DINING
ROOM CEILING APPEAR
HIGHER THAN IT
ACTUALLY IS, USING
THREE DECORATING
TECHNIQUES: SILVER
LEAFING, LIGHTING,
AND REFLECTION.

Desert Living

Photography by Naim Chidiac

In this three-story Abu Dhabi home, we were charged with creating a classic, elegant interior design for a family with four childen that follows typical Middle Eastern traditions. Materials were selected to provide light, refreshing backgrounds for living in this hot, dry, desert climate. The location near the desert means the air is always full of sand that inevitably penetrates into the homes. These rooms are very boxy, with relatively low ceiling heights, and all of the air conditioning ducts had to be camouflaged by design. By combining design techniques, we were able to give each room the illusion of more height, depth and dimension.

For example, a unique multi-level ceiling with gilding and heavily carved medallions was created to crown each room and reflect a classic style. We custom designed these ceilings to coordinate with each room's function and personality. Reflections of light from crystal chandeliers adds sparkle and interest. This culture loves detail. Wherever there was an empty wall with sufficient space, we added stone-and-mosaic fountains, combining earth and water. This is an ancient, welcoming and soothing addition to any home located near the desert.

We worked with wrought iron, stone work and frescoes, and a mixture of both Mediterranean and Arabesque shapes. The color turquoise, decorative wrought iron, and a careful melange of natural elements served as accents throughout.

"I have always loved the desert. One sits down on a
desert sand dune, sees nothing, hears nothing.
Yet through the silence something throbs, and gleams."
~ Antoine de Saint-Exupery, The Little Prince

STONE-AND-MOSAIC
FOUNTAINS, COMBINING
EARTH AND WATER. ARE
AN ANCIENT,
WELCOMING AND
SOOTHING ADDITION
TO ANY HOME LOCATED
NEAR THE DESERT.

91

"LIFE CAN ONLY BE
UNDERSTOOD BACK-
WARDS, BUT IT MUST BE
LIVED FORWARD."
~ SOREN KIERKEGAARD

A UNIQUE MULTI-
LEVELED CEILING WITH
GILDING AND HEAVILY
CARVED MEDALLIONS
WAS CREATED TO CROWN
EACH ROOM AND
REFLECT A CLASSIC STYLE.

A SOFFIT IN THE BEAMED
CEILING THAT FOLLOWS
THE CONTOURS OF THE
COUNTER VISUALLY
SEPARATES THE FAMILY
ROOM AND THE KITCHEN.

WE WORKED WITH
WROUGHT IRON, STONE
WORK, FRESCOES, AND
A MIX OF BOTH
MEDITERRANEAN AND
ARABESQUE SHAPES.

101

Harmony Castle

Photography by Naim Chidiac

This luxurious villa in Khawaneej, Dubai, is designed in the Mediterranean style. The client wanted classic elegance with backgrounds of earthtone textures and bright colors on accent pieces. Stone architraves of solid mahogany enhance all openings and doors with custom stone rosette embellishments. As you walk through the main entrance, you see the ladies' living room, with magnificent Murano glass mosaic niches hugging the room on either side of glass doors that overlook the pool.

The men's living room floor plan features a wrap-around layout with a tête-à-tête in the center, enabling the option of one or two sitting areas. Rich gold and silver leaf accents add a touch of glamour. The men's powder room features three hand-made glass vessel sinks in gold finish and custom carved cabinetry with stone columns.

The master bedroom ceilings are completely hand painted. A sitting area by the bay window gives the suite the look of a five-star hotel with all the bells and whistles. Each of the bedrooms showcases its own distinct personality reflecting the taste and lifestyle of its owner, such as the Zen bedroom, richly ornamented with espresso wood and wavy silver leaf panels throughout. In the Provence bedroom, the coziest and warmest of them all, a solid wood chateau-style bed sits in front of a padded headboard wall. Soft vanilla and mint is the flavor of this room. The Victorian bedroom is styled to fit a princess: rich yet simple and elegant. Columns on the feature wall give this room more visual interest.

"To us, our house was not unsentient matter — it had a heart,
and a soul, and eyes to see us with; and approvals and solicitudes
and deep sympathies; it was of us, and we were in its confidence,
and lived in its grace and in the peace of its benediction."
~ Mark Twain

THE CLIENT WANTED
CLASSIC ELEGANCE
WITH BACKGROUNDS OF
EARTHTONE TEXTURES
AND HIGHLIGHTS
OF GOLD.

"I CHOOSE A BLOCK OF MARBLE AND CHOP OFF WHATEVER I DON'T NEED." ~ FRANCOIS AUGUSTE RODIN

EACH OF THE BEDROOMS
WAS CUSTOMIZED FOR ITS
OWNER. WHERE IT WAS
DEEMED APPROPRIATE,
RICH GOLD AND SILVER
LEAF ACCENTS WERE
USED TO ADD A TOUCH
OF GLAMOUR.

Symphony Castle

Photography by Craig Denis

Our clients, a European family who are quite prominent in society and love to entertain frequently, wanted the ultimate in luxury in their Hollywood, Florida winter home. Classic, timeless elegance and over-sized furnishings match the overall grandeur of this home—especially the 30-foot high ceilings in the living room and in the grand foyer. We added touches of glitz and glamour in every room, large or small, through gold, silver and crystal highlights on custom trims and carved woodwork. There are also unique lighting touches including a lit-from-beneath countertop in the powder room that literally glows under a gold vessel sink.

In the grand entryway, an impressive double staircase overwhelms with beautiful scrolling ironwork. Walls are adorned with carved, silver leaf trim. The fabulous circular ceiling design sets the stage for custom ceilings that distinguish every room. Marble flooring highlighted in various shades of onyx flows throughout.

The entryway leads to an arched central gallery that extends from the central ceiling dome in each direction to connect all of the rooms with the main living areas. The formal dining room, highlighted with a priceless crystal chandelier, accommodates 20 guests comfortably. A feature wall in the master bedroom was created with custom woodwork hugging an upholstered built-in headboard highlighted with crystals. The client's special religious needs required transforming one of the bedrooms into a synagogue and creating three different kosher kitchens. The children's rooms, including a playroom on the ground floor, gave us a chance to show off our ability to match our timeless classic design in the rest of the home with whimsical spaces that continue to enchant young and old alike.

"Perfection is achieved, not when there is nothing more to add, but when there is nothing left to take away."
~Antoine de Saint-Exupéry

AN IMPRESSIVE DOUBLE
STAIRCASE OVERWHELMS
WITH ITS BEAUTIFUL
SCROLLING IRONWORK.
WALLS ARE ADORNED
WITH CARVED, SILVER
LEAF TRIM.

127

A RED ONYX FEATURE
WALL HIGHLIGHTS THE
MASTER BATH. SPIRAL
FLUTED COLUMNS
ADORN THE FOUR
CORNERS OF THE TUB.

A LIT-FROM-BENEATH
ONYX COUNTERTOP IN
THE POWDER ROOM
LITERALLY GLOWS
UNDER A GOLD
VESSEL SINK.

THE CHILDREN'S ROOMS
GAVE US A CHANCE TO
SHOW OFF OUR ABILITY
TO MATCH TIMELESS
CLASSIC DESIGN WITH
WHIMSICAL SPACES
THAT CONTINUE TO
ENCHANT YOUNG AND
OLD ALIKE.

When designing places of worship, we realize that every faith demands careful attention to details and close adherence to tradition. This family required a private synagogue within their own home, which we created out of one of the bedrooms.

The King's Castle

Photography by Craig Denis

The glass-enclosed two-story central piazza is definitely the heart and soul of this 25,000-square-foot waterfront residence located on Star Island, an exclusive residential enclave between the mainland and Miami Beach. The soothing sounds of a central fountain, positioned over a sea of blue-and-white Moroccan style tile with mosaic detailing, sets the stage in this welcoming ambiance where family and guests often gather.

In addition to the main house, the property encompasses a guest house and a gym with racquetball court and massage room. The home itself includes a "pub," a wine cellar, a music room and a billiards room. A mahogany three-sided bar highlights the fully functioning pub. A hand-painted, coffered ceiling crowns the dining room. Three crystal chandeliers, glass wall sconces and carved wood mirrors are part of the owner's private collection. We custom designed and produced almost everything else, including the buffets and the marquetry tables. The dining table can seat 30 or be separated into three separate tables, depending on the occasion.

This multi-cultural couple envisioned a home that would reflect their wordly travels. Many aspects of the design throughout the home were specifically planned to enhance and display their private collection of sculptures and paintings. In addition to professional interior design, they also wanted a fully integrated home with the latest technology that was functional but not visible. We used paint, custom coffered ceilings and custom cabinetry to camouflage electronic components, speaker grills and air conditioning vents.

"Many a book is like a key to unknown chambers
within the castle of one's own self."
~ Franz Kafka

142

146

THE OFFICE FEATURES
RICH WOOD PANELING
AND A WOOD CEILING
ADORNED WITH
HAND-CARVED CUSTOM
MOLDINGS AND RICH
ARCHITECTURAL
EMBELLISHMENTS.

161

"TRY TO LEARN
SOMETHING ABOUT
EVERYTHING AND
EVERYTHING ABOUT
SOMETHING." ~THOMAS
HENRY HUXLEY

163

The Royal Castle

Photography by Craig Denis

Guyana, bordered by Venezuela, Suriname and Brazil, is the only English speaking country in South America. It is also home to the world-famous Kaieteur Falls. We were commissioned to design the dream home for our client, one of the top gold dealers and gold producers in the country. Honoring the client's Islamic culture and traditions was very important for this couple and their three daughters. They also wanted a sense of royalty to flow throughout their home, and to have all of the interior spaces filled with richness and opulence appropriate to the family and its history. Once we got to know our clients, and they got to know us, we were honored that they gave us artistic freedom to create the interiors that they could only imagine.

Unique inserts in the marble flooring distinguish each area. A grand Romeo and Juliet staircase is detailed with hand-carved marble friezes. Two large, hand-carved, solid mahogany scrolls featuring Arabic calligraphy complement the height and drama of the entryway architecture. Both are embellished with gold leaf. Ceilings are also gold leafed and crowned with crystal chandeliers. Every room has a grand, formal look, as well as all the latest in today's technology. Yes, the technology is there; but by design, it has been carefully camouflaged in Old World palatial styling. A dividing wall between the hallway and the family room features a double-sided aquarium.

The kitchen has an over-sized island with hand-carved appliques on doors and inserts with etched designs. Even the kitchen hardware was selected with the care one would use in selecting fine jewelry, and then further embellished with crystals. Each of the three daughters' rooms has a unique princess theme with a customized bed and furnishings to complement the concept – all featuring the hand-made craftsmanship that we are known for.

"Considering that everything I see is a symphony of shapes, colors, and values, I have endless possibilities at my disposal with which to make a strong visual statement."
~Sterling Edwards

THE CLIENTS WANTED
A SENSE OF ROYALTY
TO FLOW THROUGHOUT
THEIR HOME, AND TO
HAVE ALL OF THE
INTERIOR SPACES
FILLED WITH RICHNESS
AND OPULENCE
APPROPRIATE TO THE
FAMILY AND ITS
HISTORY.

181

UNIQUE DINING CHAIR
BACKS FEATURE GOLD
DECORATIVE PANELS
THAT PROTECT AND
HIGHLIGHT RICH
DAMASK UPHOLSTERY
FABRIC.

JEWEL TONES IN THE
ARTWORK COMPLEMENT
THE OVERALL GOLDEN
GLOW OF THE FORMAL
DINING ROOM.

EVEN THE KITCHEN
HARDWARE WAS
SELECTED WITH THE
CARE ONE WOULD USE
IN SELECTING FINE
JEWELRY, AND THEN
FURTHER EMBELLISHED
WITH CRYSTALS.

"Happiness is when what you think, what you say, and what you do are in harmony."

~MAHATMA GANDHI

EACH OF THE THREE
DAUGHTERS' ROOMS
HAS A UNIQUE PRINCESS
THEME WITH A CUSTOM
BED AND FURNISHINGS
THAT COMPLEMENT
HER THEME.

ACCESSORIES ARE THE "ICING" ON THE DECORATING CAKE. THEY ARE ESPECIALLY FUN TO SHOP FOR WHEN CREATING THEME ROOMS.

HERE'S A GIRL'S ROOM
THAT CINDERELLA
WOULD BE PROUD OF!
THE "CARRIAGE" TOP
GOES UP AND DOWN
LIKE A ROMAN SHADE.

CINDERELLA'S MAGIC
CARRIAGE IS DEPICTED
IN WHIMSICAL,
COLORFUL HAND-
PAINTED WALL ART.

"WHAT'S IN A NAME?
THAT WHICH WE CALL
A ROSE BY ANY OTHER
NAME WOULD SMELL
AS SWEET." ~ WILLIAM
SHAKESPEARE

219

"YOU HAVE TO DECIDE
IF YOU'RE GOING TO
WILT LIKE A DAISY OR IF
YOU'RE JUST GOING TO GO
FORWARD AND LIVE THE
LIFE THAT YOU'VE BEEN
GRANTED."
~ KEVIN COSTNER